WHAT TO DO...

TO IMPROVE YOUR CHILD'S MANNERS

WHAT TO DO...
TO IMPROVE YOUR CHILD'S MANNERS

JOAN LEONARD

Reader's Digest

The Reader's Digest Association, Inc.
Pleasantville, N.Y./Montreal

About the Author

Joan Leonard, a contributing editor to *Parents'* magazine, has also written on parenting and manners for *Parenting, Good Housekeeping, The New York Times,* and many other publications, and is the author of a book about her experiences as a parent. The mother of a boy, 8, and a girl, 10, Leonard has taught in both middle and high schools. She and her family live on Long Island.

Consultant: Elizabeth Ellis, Ph.D., a clinical psychologist in a suburb of Atlanta, Georgia, for over 20 years, works with children, adults, and families. She has published many articles in scholarly journals and a book for parents, *Raising a Responsible Child.*

Acknowledgments

Many thanks to all the parents and children who shared their trials and tribulations about learning manners. In all cases their names have been changed to protect their privacy. My deep appreciation also goes to the many psychologists, educators, and etiquette experts who gave wise advice and practical suggestions for this book. I am especially indebted to my family—to my children, Annie and Alex, who with characteristic openness and trust allowed me to tell their stories, and to my husband, Salvatore Gentile, for his patience, love, and good humor during the writing of this book.

A Reader's Digest Book

Conceived, written, and produced by Pen & Pencil Books.
Reader's Digest Parenting Guide Series creators:
Elin McCoy (editorial); Judy Speicher (design)
Copyright © 1998 by Pen & Pencil Books LLC

Cover photograph: Scott Barrow
Photographs: 7 & 13 Stephen Simpson/FPG International LLC, 14 Bill Losh/FPG International LLC, 23 David Young-Wolff/PhotoEdit, 24 David Young-Wolff/PhotoEdit, 27 Myrleen Ferguson/PhotoEdit, 31 Nancy Sheehan/PhotoEdit, 32 Scott Barrow, Inc/stock Barrow, 34 David Young-Wolff/PhotoEdit, 37 Arthur Tilley/FPG International LLC, 39 David Young-Wolff/PhotoEdit, 41 Arthur Tilley/FPG International LLC, 47 David Madison/Tony Stone Images, 49 Paul Redman/Tony Stone Images, 55 David Young-Wolff/PhotoEdit, 61 Ron Chapple/FPG International LLC, 68 Mike Malyszko/FPG International LLC, 74 Ron Chapple/FPG International LLC, 77 Billy E. Barnes/PhotoEdit, 78 Jim Cummins/FPG International LLC, 80 Telegraph Colour Library/FPG International LLC, 83 Myrleen Ferguson/PhotoEdit, 84 Jim Cummins/FPG International LLC.

Library of Congress Cataloging in Publication Data
Leonard, Joan
    What to do... to improve your child's manners / Joan Leonard.
      p. cm. — (Reader's Digest parenting guides)
    ISBN 0-7621-0101-6
    1. Etiquette for children and teenagers. 2. Etiquette. I. Title. II. Series.
BJ1857. C5L46   1998
398. 1' 22—dc21   98-5416

CONTENTS

Between the ages of five and thirteen, our children are trying to understand and fit into their world, and this includes learning how to treat others and how to behave in a variety of social situations at home, at school, and in the world at large. In other words, they are developing the good manners they will need and use for the rest of their lives. But growing up is a slow process and so is mastering the code of behavior we call manners. Eating politely, being a good host or guest, showing respect and consideration for other people, and many other social skills take time and patience to instill in children. Along the way all kids behave rudely sometimes, and when they do, we ask ourselves questions like these:

Why does Robbie interrupt everyone? How can I get him to stop?

What will help Tina remember to say please and thank you?

Now that Jay is seven, shouldn't he be able to be polite at the dinner table?

What can I do to make Louisa and Ben behave at their grandparents' anniversary party?

How can I get Mary and Owen to write thank-you notes without a fight?

Many of us don't know what to do when our kids are rude, and we aren't sure how and when to teach them good manners. But to succeed in life, kids need to feel confident and comfortable in social situations and relationships. Having good manners helps them do that—and that's why teaching our children manners is such an essential part of parenting.

That's what this book is about

The first section, **Real Stories & Situations,** is filled with stories of parents and kids ages five to thirteen and the kinds of problems they've had with manners. In **Understanding The Problem,** you'll find answers to basic questions parents have about manners, from what they are and why they're important to why kids are sometimes rude. **What To Do** offers practical ways to teach manners to your children and includes the essentials of polite behavior at the table, on the telephone, at school, on the playing field, with friends, and more. The fourth section, **Year By Year,** is a quick reference to what manners and social skills you can expect children to learn at different ages. **We Recommend** lists the best books, games, and videos on manners to share with your children and to further your own understanding.

REAL STORIES & SITUATIONS

Is One Of These Your Child's Story?

SEAN, AGE 5

When Miranda picked up her son Sean from kindergarten, she told him they were going to stop off at his dad's new office on their way home. "Will we see Daddy's desk with my picture on it?" Sean asked, excited. Miranda said yes, amused by her son's eagerness to visit the large insurance company where his dad now worked.

Sean clung to his mom's hand on the elevator ride to the fifth floor and, as they walked to his dad's cubicle, he whispered to her, "This is a really big place."

Several co-workers standing near his dad's desk greeted Sean enthusiastically— one ruffled his hair and patted him on the back while others held out their hands for Sean to shake. Everyone seemed to be talking at once. Sean looked at the out- stretched hands but kept his own in his pockets. While his dad proudly introduced his son to his assistant and his colleagues, Sean stayed silent, his face knotted in a frown and his eyes focused on the floor. It was an awkward moment for everyone.

Miranda tried, without success, to push Sean forward, and his dad admonished him, "Come on, Sean, don't be rude. Say hello to everyone!"

But Sean stubbornly refused to budge. Finally his dad's colleagues said they had to get back to work. Miranda and her husband exchanged puzzled glances. Sean was usually such an outgoing, friendly child.

AUDREY, AGE 6

A new family moved in next door to the Brody family. Audrey, thrilled that it included a girl her age, invited Betsy over to play on Saturday afternoon.

Shortly after Betsy and her mom arrived, Betsy announced, "I want something to eat," opened the refrigerator, and looked inside to see what was there.

Eager to be accommodating to her daughter's new friend, Mrs. Brody offered peanut butter, crackers, pretzels, and juice.

But Betsy wrinkled her nose and demanded, "What kind of peanut butter?" When she saw the brand, she said, "I hate that kind and I hate pretzels." Betsy's mother sighed, "She's a very fussy eater."

Audrey said nervously, "Do we have anything else, Mommy? Could we have cream cheese and crackers?"

Betsy frowned and said, "I hate cream cheese, too! I want cookies."

Audrey's mom hesitated. It was a family rule not to have sweets between meals— and her daughter knew that. But she wanted Audrey to make friends with Betsy, so she looked in the cupboard, pulled out a bag, and said, "Okay. How about Oreos?"

Betsy grabbed the bag, then said to Audrey, "Great. Show me your room and we'll eat them there."

Audrey knew her bedroom was off- limits for eating. What should she do? She looked at her mom.

DANNY, AGE 7

Danny, his parents, his little brother, and his grandparents finally finished eating the special cake in the shape of a cowboy hat that Danny's grandma had baked for his seventh birthday. As the grown-ups talked, Danny looked longingly at the big box his grandparents had brought for him. "Isn't it time to open my present?" he asked. He was pretty sure it was the robot game he really, really wanted. The last time he had talked to his grandpa on the phone, Danny had told him all about it.

But when Danny opened the box and pushed aside the tissue paper, he found a yellow slicker with a matching rimmed hat for rainy days. He stared at it in disbelief. "Oh, no," he cried. "I didn't want clothes! Clothes don't count as a present!"

His grandma, upset, said defensively, "But you need a raincoat! I thought you would like it."

"Well, I don't!" Danny retorted. "I thought you'd get me that robot game." And he ran out of the room.

Danny's parents were mortified. What had come over their usually polite son who loved his grandparents? "Danny!" his father called after him. "Come back here right now and thank Nanna and Grandpa!"

But Danny had gone outside to ride his bike. The family watched through the picture window as he pedaled as fast as he could down the driveway.

BILLY, AGE 8

Ann Sampson's new boss invited the Sampson family to dinner to celebrate Ann's promotion. Ann's boss had kids, too—twin boys a year younger than Billy and a daughter the same age as Billy's sister, Emma, who was ten. It would be informal, a way to get acquainted, he told Ann.

But dinner turned out to be much fancier than Ann or her husband, Bob, thought it would be. In the large formal dining room a lace tablecloth and crystal candlesticks graced a table set with good china. Ann was suddenly apprehensive about how her children would behave.

The kids were seated across the table from Ann and Bob, who watched Billy eyeing the mashed potatoes (his favorite!) and turkey. Then Ann's boss and his family bowed their heads, crossed themselves, and began, "Bless us, O Lord. . ."

The Sampsons never said grace before meals, but Bob and Ann bowed their heads, too. Billy, however, suddenly started giggling. Horrified, Ann gave him a stern look, but Billy giggled even louder. While the family continued the prayer, Ann watched helplessly as Billy actually served himself some mashed potatoes and gulped some of his soda.

"Do you have to do that every night?" he asked the twins when grace was finished. Both boys nodded. "Well, it sure took a long time," Billy declared, looking around the table. "Can someone pass the gravy?"

BECKY, AGE 9

Becky had spent all morning phoning various friends to find someone who could come over—with no luck. Several hadn't been home, so she had left messages on their answering machines to call her back. As a last resort, she tried her least favorite friend, Alexis—a classmate she thought was boring but better than no one. Alexis was free! "I'll be over in about an hour," she promised Becky.

But as luck would have it, Becky's best friend, Julia, called just fifteen minutes later, home from soccer practice at last. "Our new swimming pool is ready!" she announced to Becky. "My mom says you can come over for a swim this afternoon."

Elated, Becky said, "Sure! I'll ask my mom and call you right back."

Becky explained the situation to her mother and then added, "I want to go to Julia's, but I don't really want to hurt Alexis's feelings, even though I don't like her very much. So, will you call Alexis and tell her not to come over so I can go to Julia's and swim?"

"Oh, Becky, this isn't the right thing to do," her mother began in protest.

"Mom, please? I can't think of a good excuse for Alexis," Becky pleaded as she handed the phone to her mother.

SARAH, AGE 10

Sarah, an only child, was used to talking to grown-ups and had no trouble expressing ideas and strong opinions to others. In fact, her parents had always encouraged this. So they were upset and puzzled by Sarah's latest report card. On it her home-room teacher, Mrs. Owen, had written, "Sarah is very mature and intelligent for her age and her desire to help other children is commendable. But she irritates both teachers and other children with her frequent interruptions and corrections. Let's meet and discuss this."

The day before the conference, Sarah's mom finally understood what Mrs. Owen was concerned about when she overheard Sarah and Cassie, a girl who lived down the street, talking by the front porch.

"This is my new bike," said Cassie proudly. "My dad gave it to me for my birthday and—"

"That's cool," interrupted Sarah, "except that it doesn't have a holder for a water bottle. Mine does, see?" She pointed.

"Yeah, but—" began Cassie.

"And your reflector isn't big enough. You could have an accident," Sarah added.

"Well, my dad says it's okay and—"

"Don't worry, I'll tell you where to get a better one. My mom has the information." And Sarah dashed into the house.

Her mom saw that Cassie had turned away and was biking back to her own house. Was Sarah like this with her teachers, too? her mom wondered. What could they do to make Sarah see how rude she was being to others?

DAVID, AGE 11

"I have to drive downtown to mail this package and do some errands," David's dad told him. "I'll be back in an hour or two. Your mom will be back about five o'clock. Now remember, don't answer the door, no friends over, and—"

"And take phone messages because you're expecting an important call. I know, I know," David said with a grin. "All I'm going to do is play my video games."

Just as David reached level six in his game, the phone rang.

"What!" David said impatiently into the portable phone, one thumb still working the game controls.

The voice on the other end of the phone asked hesitantly, "Is your dad there?"

"No, he's not," David replied absently, his eyes glued to his video game on the television screen. Maybe he was going to win this game at last!

"How about your mom?"

"She's not here, either. Call back later," David said grumpily, hung up, and went back to his game.

When David's dad returned an hour later, he asked David whether there had been any calls.

"Yeah, somebody called just when I was about to win my game," he responded.

"Who was it?" his dad asked. "Am I supposed to call back?"

"No clue," David answered cheerfully, and he turned up the volume of his game.

MAGGIE, AGE 12

Maggie's next-door neighbor, Beth Murphy, was an English teacher at the local junior high school, and she was also best friends with Maggie's mom. Consequently, ever since she could remember, Maggie had called her, Beth.

On the day she started junior high, Maggie was a little nervous, but just after sixth period, she saw Beth walking down the hall with the principal and two ninth graders. It seemed weird to see Beth in her different role as a teacher.

"Hi, Beth," Maggie called out. A few heads turned, and the principal, surprised and not pleased, looked over at Beth.

"Hello, Maggie," said Beth. "Let me walk you to your locker." Beth excused herself and accompanied Maggie down the hall. Then she said gently, "Maggie, please remember to call me Mrs. Murphy when we're in school."

"Oh, sure, no problem," Maggie answered and waved good-bye to Beth as she turned into the faculty lounge.

But Maggie was hurt. All of a sudden it seemed that she had done something wrong, but she wasn't sure what it was. This was Beth, her mom's best friend! Didn't she like Maggie anymore?

STUART, AGE 13

Each Friday after school, the Hopewell Middle School Chess Club sponsored chess games in Mr. Rictor's classroom, and today was the championship round. All the kids gathered around the finalists, Stuart and Les, who were concentrating fiercely on the board in front of them. Since Stuart had managed to acquire more pieces than Les, it looked like he would win. But suddenly Les moved his queen up several spaces, closing in on Stuart's king.

"Checkmate!" he yelled triumphantly.

Stuart stared at the board. Les was right. He had lost the game.

A combination of humiliation and disappointment flooded over Stuart. He had always been a better player than Les, and he never expected to lose. In frustration he hit the board with his fist, sending some of the pieces flying off the table.

"Hey, watch it," said Les good-naturedly as he picked up several pawns. "It was a close game, and you played great."

"Yeah, I know," said Stuart mournfully. "I would have won, too, if everybody hadn't been so noisy," he added bitterly,

The other kids looked at one another. They thought they had been extremely quiet. In fact, Mr. Rictor was a stickler for keeping silent while others were playing and reminded everyone before each game.

"They broke my concentration," Stuart insisted, his arms folded across his chest. "And they were standing closer to me than to you. I couldn't even think straight. Otherwise I wouldn't have lost."

Les didn't know what to say, so he didn't answer. He just gathered the rest of the chess pieces into the box while Stuart stomped out the door. ❏

UNDERSTANDING THE PROBLEM

Answers To Basic Questions

What Are Manners?

It's easy to say what manners are when we see our kids displaying *bad* manners. For example, your family and relatives are sitting around the Thanksgiving dinner table and your son uses his index finger to help himself to some cranberry sauce or your daughter entertains the troops by making milk come out of her nose. If you're like me, you're so embarrassed by your own children's behavior that you're almost relieved when your sister's two children start a burping contest. At moments like these parents are quick to recognize what good manners AREN'T.

Most of us want our kids to have *good* manners, even if we're not sure just what that means for children today and what's reasonable to expect at ages five or ten or thirteen. While we all know that being polite is much more than sitting quietly at the dinner table and knowing which fork to use for dessert, many of us aren't so sure about what specifics are still essential for our children to know.

But if we understand what good and bad manners are, the reasons behind them, and why they're so important, we can begin to focus on the ones that matter.

Manners are based on courtesy

When I asked my eight-year-old son what he thought good manners were, he reflected a moment and then said quite seriously, "Not farting in front of people because they don't like it?" Okay, I asked for that one. But I have to admit that my son had the right idea. Much of what we call good manners is simply common sense and common courtesy toward other people. When six-year-old Nate has a cold, he

won't spread germs to the rest of the family if he blows his nose into a tissue or covers his mouth when he coughs. That's not only more sanitary, it's also good manners because it's showing consideration for others.

At the dinner table, we ask children to pass the gravy so that everyone gets a portion without having to reach and bump into the person sitting next to him or knock over a glass of water or two. On the bus, when Naomi gives up her seat to a disabled or elderly person, she is being thoughtful and kind.

On the other hand, interrupting adult conversations, bragging about a new pair of Rollerblades, and cutting in the popcorn line at the movies are all ways of being discourteous to others—and as a result, they're *bad* manners.

In most situations, showing sensitivity and thoughtfulness toward another person is also showing *good* manners, and once our children understand this, they're on the right track.

A code of behavior

Many of the specific ways we show consideration for others stem from a code of rules with arbitrary elements that depend on the particular culture we live in. In ours, chewing with your mouth closed and saying excuse me when you burp are considered polite behavior, but in other cultures, as preteens often remind us, they are not.

Think about all the areas of kids' lives this code of manners touches. There are polite ways to meet and greet people, to answer and speak on the telephone, to eat at home or in a restaurant, to show sportsmanship on the playing field, to deal with friends, teachers, and other adults, to behave in other people's homes, at school, and in public places, and even to dress, thank someone for a present, or leave a party. As parents learn, most of these behaviors don't come naturally to children. No wonder they forget them!

Of course, the rules kids follow at an unsupervised table in the cafeteria usually reflect their own culture instead of ours, and sometimes that's appropriate. But if children throw a fit when they lose a board game or fail to thank the party host, they are judged impolite by others—and their parents are judged, too.

A set of social skills

Manners also include key social skills— like knowing how to talk to people, give compliments, share willingly, be sensitive to how someone else is feeling, and be warm, friendly, and tolerant. These help children navigate social life and relationships successfully, something that's highly important to elementary- and middle-school kids. Julie, for example, had never known anyone confined to a wheelchair until a new boy entered her fifth-grade class. No one knew what to say to him. But because Julie's parents had taught her to be kind to others as well as tolerant and accepting of anyone, no matter how different, she was able to look directly at the new boy, smile naturally, and say, "Hi!"

A form of self-control

As most of us quickly realize, good manners depend on self-control—and that's why kids' ages dictate what we can expect from them. Two-year-old Ethan can't understand (or remember) the concept of not sticking his finger up his nose. And requiring a preschooler to sit at the dinner table listening to adult conversation for thirty minutes is a recipe for disaster. But by the time children are three years old, they are starting to learn how to manage themselves— to use words instead of hitting, to share the cookies instead of grabbing them. By ages five or six, they can exercise more

self-control, and we ask them to take small bites, hold in their ideas until it's their turn to talk, and keep their observations about the size of a fat neighbor to themselves.

For special occasions

Most children can sense that they'd better use all that "manners stuff," as my son puts it, on a special day or occasion. Just getting dressed up encourages good behavior. At my parents' fiftieth wedding anniversary recently, for example, my extended family gathered at a very fancy restaurant to celebrate. My two children were decked out in their finest apparel—a spiffy new blazer with a tie for my son, and a pale yellow silk dress with matching headband for my ten-year-old daughter. On the way to the restaurant they bickered loudly in the back seat over who got to hold the present and who got to hold the card, and my husband and I prayed they would settle down in front of my relatives—some of whom I hadn't seen in years.

At the party, however, their manners were impeccable. They congratulated my parents, gave them the present and big hugs, then walked back to their seats and put their napkins on their laps.

For daily life

Unfortunately, my children's wonderful manners disappeared the moment we returned home, and by the next morning

> ▶ PARENT TIPS

> ▶ "Our family has this secret code in public," says Marissa, a single mom of 3 boys. "If my kids see my eyebrows shoot up at the same time I yank on my ear—in church or at the supermarket, for example—they *know* they're on 'bad manners' territory. This works much better than yelling at them in front of their friends."

we were back to daily life. My son was eating Froot Loops out of the box and my daughter was trying to grab the cereal out of his hand without success. "You pig!" she shrieked. "You're the pig," he responded. "Soo—eee," he added maliciously. (These lapses, of course, are completely normal.)

Manners are good habits, the basic ground rules for everyday life. In order for them to become second nature, though, kids have to practice them regularly in everyday situations—and that means at breakfast with siblings as well as in school and with friends.

Manners are ancient

Many people are surprised to learn that the concept of good manners has been with us for centuries, even millennia. The ancient Egyptians were actually writing books on etiquette as early as 2000 B.C. In fact, the word "etiquette" goes back to the Middle Ages. It comes from the French word *l'estiquette*—loosely translated "ticket"—which referred to the list of rules for behavior toward the nobility that were posted in feudal villages throughout England and Europe. One rule, for example, required peasant boys and men to tip their hats when greeting anyone considered above them in class or station in life. Some regulations were adjusted now and then—often at the whim of the king—but eventually the foundations of the etiquette we now use emerged.

Manners have evolved

What we consider good manners for children has changed over time and continues to change. Some rules children followed in the past seem surprising to us now. At the turn of this century, for example, school-children always stood up to answer a question when the teacher called on them. Upper-class girls—and those aspiring to be—curtsied when meeting an adult. Boys tipped hats to elders, and children were considered extremely rude if they spoke at any social function unless they were first addressed by one of the adults. (Remember the old saying, "Children should be seen and not heard"?)

Rigid rules of etiquette eased up substantially after World War I and again after World War II, and by the time the baby-boomer generation came along, most children were raised with a let-it-all-hang-out attitude. Self-expression had become highly important, and many thought a polite, well-mannered child ran the risk of becoming psychologically damaged—or at least would suffer from stifled creativity!

Now interest in teaching good manners to kids is back, but in a more common-sense way. Children no longer have to curtsy or tip their hat, but most parents have come to recognize that teaching kids basic consideration for others and imparting simple rules for how to treat them is an important part of their education. ❏

Why Do Kids Need Good Manners?

ASK THE EXPERTS

• Dr. Elizabeth Ellis, an Atlanta-based family therapist and author of *Raising a Responsible Child* (Birch Lane Press, 1996), says good manners are essentially good people skills. "The troubled kids I see in treatment are those who never learned those basic people skills; they're impulsive, thoughtless, self-absorbed, and not aware of how their behavior affects others."

As parents, we want our children to succeed. We want them to grow up to achieve their goals, to have someone to love who loves them, and to live happy and productive lives. In order to do this, we teach them survival skills and try to provide them with as many advantages as possible. We applaud at their piano recitals and cheer at their soccer games to show our support. We check homework, supply state-of-the-art computers, and sign kids up for after-school activities. We give them chores around the house to teach responsibility and a weekly allowance to teach the value of money.

But in addition to all this, our kids also need a set of rules to help them know how to behave during all of the above activities as well as in their social life. Manners are those rules.

Rules help kids remember

Between the ages of five and thirteen, children are trying to understand and fit into their world. Most of them are highly aware that there are right and wrong ways to do things, and they really *do* want to do things the right way—most of the time. All kids enjoy favorite games and sports when the rules are clearly laid out, and they work hard to learn and follow the rules of new ones. In games, as in daily life, rules help them remember what to do. Since kids don't always know what's appropriate in every situation, they're usually relieved when grown-ups set limits—as long as these are reasonable—to keep them on track. Of course, they also complain about these limits.

Being liked

All our kids want to be liked, and having good manners makes them more likable to everyone—both adults and other children. That's one of the most powerful reasons to teach them manners. When you think about it, who wouldn't prefer to spend time with someone like eight-year-old Linda, who compliments friends, greets them cheerfully at the bus, listens when they're telling a story, and generally makes them feel good by being considerate of their feelings?

Manners can help children make and keep friends, smooth over awkward moments, minimize misunderstandings, help solve conflicts, and make it easier for them to get along with others. Kids who have good manners, like Linda, are pleasant to be around. It's also more pleasant for parents to live with children who treat us courteously—at least some of the time.

Feeling confident

When she was five, my daughter became suddenly apprehensive as we arrived at a classmate's birthday party but then said bravely, "I know what to do." The sure-fire etiquette rules we'd reviewed beforehand were simple and basic, but just recalling and reciting them to herself made her feel more confident: say "Happy Birthday;" hand your present to Karen or her mom; say hello to the other children; say thank you when you get a piece of cake; say no thanks if you don't like the food, and say thank you when you leave.

No matter what their age, children feel more comfortable and secure in a situation when they know the rules. That includes middle schoolers heading out to a party.

Knowing they can make people feel good and knowing what to do in social situations also gives kids a boost of confidence in themselves and their own abilities. And that translates into self-esteem.

Helping kids get what they want

There are plenty of other obvious benefits to good manners. If you were a librarian, for example, which child described below would you go out of your way to help?

Gerry, a fifth grader, stood by the circulation desk, waited until the librarian was off the phone, and then said, "Excuse me, Mrs. Milman, could you please tell me where the books about the Middle Ages are?" Debbie, on the other hand, interrupted Mrs. Milman's conversation with another student to demand loudly, "Hey! Mrs. Milman. I have to have a book on the Middle Ages right now!"

The truth is, the child with the good manners is the one who usually gets what he or she wants: the party invitations; the teacher's good will; the coach's extra help; a chance to go camping with another family; the attention of the opposite sex; the job interview; and, ultimately, the job.

Making a good impression

Unfortunately, we're all judged by the first impressions we make, and so are our children. That's one reason we try to keep them reasonably groomed with hair combed, hands washed, and neat, clean clothes. But first impressions include behavior as well as appearance.

The other day my daughter's new friend waltzed into my bedroom without knocking and started brushing her hair with my hairbrush. I took it away from her as gently as possible, but I could see by her bewildered expression that she didn't know she had done anything wrong. She may turn out to be the nicest, kindest friend my daughter has, but her lack of manners colored my impression of her.

If I hear my son's playmate shouting obscene words, I form an impression of this child *and* his parents. Do his parents talk like that at home? I wonder. Probably not—crude language is everywhere these days—but my judgment sticks.

A child who has good manners, however, creates a lasting *positive* impression. ❑

ADVICE FROM KIDS

How does having good manners help you?

○ "By being polite at my friend's house—like taking my shoes off when I go in their living room and carrying my plate to the kitchen after dinner—I get invited back as much as I want," reports Zack, 10.

○ "When I ask to go shopping with my grandma, she usually says yes. She told me that it's because I always say please and thank you," offers Jenny, 7.

Why Are Kids Rude?

On a day when your child—and his friends—can't seem to muster a please or a thank you or, worse, when the teacher calls to inform you that your son or daughter talked back rudely to the principal, you may be convinced that being rude is the way kids naturally behave. Like many parents, you probably ask yourself, Why are children so rude? Are they deliberately trying to provoke or are they unaware of what they're doing?

It may come as a relief to know that all children behave rudely sometimes, and there are many reasons why they do. It usually helps to understand the cause when we're trying to figure out how to correct their behavior.

What is being rude?

At the age of five, most children define rudeness as "something grown-ups don't like." Only later do they graduate to "something that makes someone else feel bad." Very often being rude means doing something you shouldn't, as was the case with eleven-year-old Vincent and his three friends at the movie theater. They annoyed several people in the audience, especially those sitting right behind them, by imitating the rat-a-tat of gunfire on the soundtrack, whispering to one another, noisily chomping on popcorn, and frequently standing up and pushing along the row to the aisle so they could head out to the concession in the lobby and bring back more popcorn. But sometimes kids are being rude when they *don't* do something they should, such as hold open the door for an elderly neighbor at the supermarket.

Kids in elementary and middle school know that there are rude words, rude tones of voice, and rude actions. The trouble is, they frequently forget because they don't stop to think!

A matter of age and development

Some reasons for rudeness vary with age and stage of social development. Often a young child's rudeness is completely unintentional. While standing in line with her mom at the supermarket, five-year-old Alison noticed the very fat woman behind them and asked in a loud voice, "Mommy, why does that lady have three chins?"

This is just the kind of question that parents dread. The woman glared at Alison,

▶ PARENT TIPS

▶ "When our son began 4th grade, he was rude to his younger sister every day after school. Gradually we found out that 2 of his older classmates were 'dissing' him on the playground. By the time he came home he wanted to get even with someone, in our case his own sister," says Kate, mother of a 10-year-old and a 7-year-old.

everyone else in line averted his or her eyes, and Alison's mother, mortified by her daughter's rudeness, was unable, like most of us, to think of the right thing to say. To Alison, though, her question was perfectly reasonable—she doesn't yet have the sensitivity to others to know when her words will hurt them.

A period of rudeness is common for five-, six-, and sometimes seven-year-olds, who blurt out insults and indulge in name-calling to celebrate their growing linguistic skill, especially when they're angry.

Younger children also have a more limited awareness of manners than older ones do. A ten-year-old, for example, usually knows it's rude to interrupt an adult conversation at a dinner. But a five-year-old jumps in without thinking.

Then there are preteens. Almost overnight, most parents complain, their children seem to become rude and inconsiderate of others. Like Vincent's dad, parents find themselves saying several times a day, "Don't speak to me like that!" It helps to remember that normal banter between preteens is full of language that adults find offensive. It often spills over into family life because kids this age are testing limits to find out what's acceptable and what's not.

Being self-centered

Often kids don't realize they are being rude because they aren't thinking of anyone but themselves. We all know that toddlers honestly believe the entire world revolves around them. We forget that learning to think about how your behavior affects others—the most basic tenet of etiquette—takes a long time. Kids of all ages—and adults—can be thoughtless, and have to be reminded that other people's feelings count, too. Young teens are notoriously insecure, and that sometimes causes them to be self-absorbed to the point of ignoring others altogether. Vincent and his friends at the movies weren't trying deliberately to ruin the movie for the people behind them; in fact, they weren't thinking about them at all! Instead, they were celebrating how good it felt to be part of a group.

A reaction to stress

When kids are repeatedly and deliberately rude, they may be trying to tell us something is not right in their lives. Rudeness at home is a way of letting off steam. Maybe our children's feelings are getting hurt at school. Maybe they are under a lot of pressure academically or in sports. Some, especially young ones, are rude when they are uncomfortable, tired, need exercise, or are spending too much time in front of the TV.

They don't know the rules

Sometimes kids are rude because they haven't been taught what's appropriate in a particular situation. Often the problem is that we've given them instructions that are too vague, like "Be polite!" or haven't spelled out our specific expectations, as in "Now that we're in a car pool, I expect you to thank the driver when you get out." If we don't prepare kids for situations and teach them the right way to do something, we can't be too surprised at how they behave. One enterprising parent I know keeps a list of basic civilized behavior posted on the family bulletin board.

When kids are angry

During recess, Scott, a third grader, plays soccer with a group of boys. When a teammate misses a pass, Scott loses the opportunity to kick in the winning goal and explodes in anger. "You moron," he yells at his teammate in disgust. "You're such a butt-brain!" Eventually a teacher's aide makes him leave the playing field.

Kids who have trouble managing anger, like Scott, are often rude. When preteens are deliberately rude to wound their parents or provoke a fight with them, the reason is usually anger. It helps to find out *why* kids are angry, but unless they learn to control their anger and handle frustration without hurting others, this may become their habitual response to every annoyance.

Challenging authority

Deliberate rudeness to adults is also a way of asserting independence and challenging their authority. Ten-year-old Caroline, like many girls her age, takes a sarcastic, scornful, disrespectful tone when talking to her mother, partly to show off in front of her friends and partly to let her mom know she's growing up. (This doesn't mean her mom should allow this, however!) Some preteens rebel against what they view as phony and superficial rules.

Following Mom's or Dad's lead

We've all heard it a hundred times: the best way to get a child to do what you want is to be a good example. With all the stresses of modern parenthood, we know that is easier said than done. But children imitate whoever is closest to them, as Scott did. Each morning Scott's dad drives him to school, and Scott watches his normally even-tempered father turn into Monster Driver as soon as he hits rush-hour traffic. His father honks his horn angrily if the car ahead of him doesn't leap into gear the second the light turns green and uses obscene language, calling out to drivers phrases that are just as rude as the ones Scott uses on the soccer field when *he* gets angry.

If you and your spouse are rude to one another, your children will probably be rude to their siblings and friends, too. The good news, however, is that if they see you speaking politely to each other as well as to others on a daily basis—for example, to a waitress ("May I please have the hamburger plate without coleslaw?") or on the telephone ("Sorry, we're not interested in having our basement inspected.")—they'll imitate that behavior, too!

Peer pressure

Have you ever watched a group of twelve-year-old boys eating in someone's family room—perhaps your own? Even a child who usually puts a napkin on his lap, makes polite conversation with his parents about his day, and places his utensils on the plate before clearing it, will be right there with his friends, shoving food into his mouth while giggling, spraying soda, making rude noises, and using language you'd rather not hear.

No matter what your child's age, peer pressure can encourage him to be rude in ways he probably wouldn't be if he was alone or with you. Just so you know: this is normal. Kids usually recover their manners when Grandma comes to visit.

Rudeness is everywhere

Not only do kids mimic their parents' behavior, they also are products of their culture. And these days, our kids see plenty of examples of rudeness every single day. Television sitcoms feature characters that trade vulgar insults, and body functions are usually the punch line to their jokes. Even major-league ice hockey, baseball, and basketball players—revered as heroes

by many kids—now often scream epithets at umpires and make obscene gestures to the camera.

It's no wonder that children aren't always sure what's okay and what's not and get the idea that they have the right to be rude to others, too.

Nobody's perfect

Of course, when your child behaves badly at home, it's worth reminding yourself that children usually save their very worst behavior for their parents! ❏

What About Being Fresh & Talking Back?

"Mark, please sit up straight at the table," his dad says quietly.

"Why should I?" Mark retorts. "You slouch, too. All I ever hear at dinner is 'Mark, sit up straight.'" This last sentence is said in a sarcastic, singsong tone.

"MARK! No backchat or you'll go to your room!"

If you're like most parents, few things are as annoying as a "fresh" child. Even level-headed, rational parents sometimes lose control with a child who has to have the last word or who pokes fun at a parental comment. Talking back the way Mark did throws down the gauntlet in a kind of challenge, so that his dad has to take some kind of action to stop it, or try to ignore it.

What is being fresh?

Fresh kids are smart alecks and often know-it-alls, too. Usually "being fresh" means a disrespectful verbal bantering or bold sassiness with adults that pushes them to the limit of their tolerance. Most of us know it when we hear it but find it hard to define. It includes talking back, arguing, heavy-handed sarcasm, not accepting "no" from adults, and refusing to do something you've been asked to do, all delivered with plenty of what today is called "attitude." Typically, fresh kids eventually do what you ask, but insist on their own twist or condition. A fresh kid like Mark knows exactly what he's doing—he intends to provoke. Mind you, there is no actual rebellion. But parents find themselves responding, "WHAT DID YOU SAY?"

Why are kids fresh?

For some kids the problem is inborn temperament—they're simply predisposed to be stubborn and challenge authority. For others, sassing or making fun of an adult is a way to show off and a way to put adults on notice that kids can be in control, too. Movies and television exaggerate this kind of behavior and hold it up as humorous, thus offering them innumerable lessons in how to be fresh. Some fresh kids have parents who assert their opinions in an outspoken way and actively encourage their kids to do the same—though most draw a line over tone, the manner in which it's done, and how long it goes on. Still other children are defiant to cover up their feelings of failure in school.

As a middle-school teacher for many years, I've observed that the child who usually says, "Chapter Four? That's too long to do for homework!" is usually the same one who says sarcastically to a cafeteria worker, "You call that mashed potatoes?"

Nip it in the bud

Like most experts, Paula Person, who teaches etiquette programs throughout the country and abroad, urges parents to stop fresh behavior by sitting down with their children and explaining that this is not showing respect for others. If children get away with fresh remarks, it's harder to dis-cipline the same behavior the next time.

Tolerance for fresh behavior varies considerably from parent to parent, but it's considered rude—and usually criticized—by teachers, coaches, and other adults in kids' lives. If they perceive your child as sassy, they'll be more likely to find fault with his or her behavior and work.

Set standards and consequences

Experts suggest parents let kids know what kinds of backtalk won't be tolerated. Imagine these two scenarios:

Scene #1: "It's eight o'clock, time for bed," Cynthia says to her daughter, Vicky.

"Can't I stay up to watch this program?"

"No, Vicky, I know you're tired."

"No, I'm not. You're tired!" she mutters.

Cynthia sighs and pretends not to have heard. "I said it's time for bed. Come on," she begs her daughter. "Don't you know what time it is?" she adds sternly.

"I can tell time. Can you?" Vicky says belligerently.

Scene #2: "It's eight o'clock—bedtime."

"Can't I stay up to watch this program?"

"You know the rules. Let's go, Vicky."

"But—"

"Vicky, if you keep talking back every night, bedtime will be seven-thirty."

In Scene #2 Cynthia sets an important standard. She successfully prevents an opportunity for talking back by refusing to get pulled into an argument and by restating the rules. Vicky knows that if she continues, she'll have to pay a consequence.

It's always worth discussing with a child just why you don't like this kind of behavior. Help children figure out how to be assertive and independent in ways that don't offend people, and to assess when it's better to hold their tongues and humor someone in authority. ❏

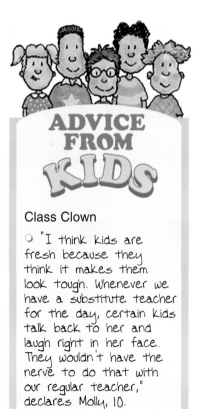

ADVICE FROM KIDS

Class Clown

○ "I think kids are fresh because they think it makes them look tough. Whenever we have a substitute teacher for the day, certain kids talk back to her and laugh right in her face. They wouldn't have the nerve to do that with our regular teacher," declares Molly, 10.

How Do Kids Develop Manners?

Every day in the school cafeteria, Amanda, a fourth grader, opens her lunchbox and spreads the contents out on the table. It usually includes a bag of potato chips or chocolate chip cookies, and she automatically offers these to the five friends she regularly sits with before taking any herself. Her pal Mary next to her, however, keeps most of her food inside her lunch bag—the cupcake, for example, is never taken out, apparently for fear that someone will ask for a piece. Her hand slowly goes into the bag, she breaks off a piece, then pops it into her mouth.

What makes Mary and Amanda behave so differently? Are some kids just born generous, kind, giving, and mannerly and others selfish and fearful?

That's partially true, but many experts believe that kids develop most of their behavior—including both good and bad manners—through example, experience, and instruction.

Your beliefs about manners are key

Amanda's parents believe it is good manners to share food with others and have taught their children that belief in many ways. Though Mary's parents insist on napkins on laps, they don't consider sharing food a priority. Kids develop a set of manners just as they develop a set of tastes in foods—tuna casserole versus fried squid—from their own family's example.

Whatever manners are considered important at home are the ones children tend to pick up and use themselves—for better or for worse.

The beginnings of manners

Home is the place where kids first learn about love, about caring, and about pleasing others. Most young children, like four-year-old Daisy, want very much to please Mom and Dad—and that's one of the first steps in learning to think about others and thus in developing manners.

Daisy's parents are careful to let her know how her efforts make them feel. Her dad says, "That was very thoughtful and kind of you, Daisy," when she brings him the newspaper. Her mom smiles and praises her for saying hello and shaking hands with a family friend who has dropped by for coffee. As a result, Daisy is learning to be sensitive to others' feelings and to grasp that her actions have an effect on other people—in other words, she is beginning to develop empathy.

Researchers have found that children who have empathy usually show more concern and consideration for others. So by encouraging empathy, parents are setting the stage for good manners—which means children, perhaps with a little prodding, will understand that sending a thank-you note to Aunt Grace will make her feel good or that it's not very nice to ignore your

a two-year-old throws food in a restaurant or hits a friend—all are preludes to the manners we want kids to display at older ages. Experts agree that even a three-year-old can learn to say please and thank you. Building on these simple early actions and words, a child adds on skills as he or she becomes more aware of what manners are.

cousin Tim at a family party, even if you don't feel like playing with someone who is only five years old, because it will hurt his feelings.

Manners develop at a young age

In the first several years of a child's life, experts tell us, his or her patterns of relating to others are being set in place. That's why your son or daughter is absorbing some of the basics of manners long before you are actively trying to teach them. Helping a baby wave bye-bye to a visitor, wiping a one-year-old's hands before she eats lunch, saying no in a stern way when

Manners must be taught

No matter what they absorb, however, children don't develop manners instinctively as they do other skills such as crawling. Like reading, consideration for others and specific manners such as putting a napkin in your lap require deliberate instruction— my grandmother used to compare teaching manners to children with training a puppy.

When you think about it, this makes perfect sense. Like puppies, our kids don't always know the right thing to do. So it's up to parents to make suggestions like

AGE FACTOR

❖ According to psychologist Elizabeth Ellis, children don't fully learn to think from the viewpoint of another person until they reach the age of 11 or 12. "We all start out as egocentric little creatures, and it takes us that long a time to develop multiple points of view," she says.

ADVICE FROM KIDS

Learning the hard way

○ "One time when our family went out to dinner, I snapped my fingers at a waitress to get her attention—I saw someone do that in a TV show once. She came over and whispered in my ear that I was rude, that instead I should raise my arm when I see a waitress. I was so embarrassed I never did it again," says Adam, 13.

"When Johnny arrives for your party, he would probably appreciate it if you introduced him to your school friends because he won't know anybody."

And in many cases manners go *against* kids' natural instincts. After all, why shouldn't you pop up and down when you feel like it at dinner or wander around with a chicken leg in your hand? Adults may automatically take a message when someone phones, but this isn't a high priority for a child on his way to the playroom to build a fort with his friend.

How experiences count

Most nights of the week, Joe, age eight, and his sister Kate, age eleven, eat dinner with their parents, and every Friday the family heads for a local Chinese restaurant. The kids are now adept at eating with chopsticks. With all this practice in eating with adults, it's not surprising that Joe and Kate have pretty good table manners and are comfortable eating at friends' homes as well as under their grandparents' eagle eyes during an occasional Sunday dinner.

Joe's sportsmanship has improved with every season of soccer and Little League tournaments. Thanks to attendance at puppet shows when they were little, annual excursions to see *The Nutcracker Suite* ballet, and regular family movie nights, both have learned, over the years, good audience behavior. Now Kate is

allowed to attend boy-girl parties, and she is learning to pretend to have fun when she's bored and not to gossip (at least not too much) about who likes whom.

The moral: children's manners also develop when we expose them to many experiences where they have an opportunity to learn new skills and to practice the ones already in their repertory. That means traveling to new locations, sleeping over at friends' houses, being involved in religious services, visiting your office for a day, attending special events, and much more.

A long-term project

Growing up is a process, and so is the development of manners. Nothing can turn a child overnight into a polite, kind individual who thinks of others, and progress can be very uneven. At six years of age, Melanie was an inveterate interrupter. Now, at ten, after what her mother is sure have been five thousand reminders, she is not, most of the time. Sam astonished his dad by writing page-long thank-you notes to his grandpa at age eight, but now, at age thirteen, he says, "It's hypocritical to thank somebody for a present I don't like," and disdains writing anything at all unless his dad nags him to.

Manners are learned a little bit at a time. The basics become the building blocks of more complex and sophisticated rules as our children grow up. ❏

Some outgoing children, like Tina, seem to have good people skills from an early age. Now ten, Tina has a knack for making other children, not just her friends, feel comfortable. She's the first to smile, introduce herself, and start a conversation, she shares her possessions generously—except with her little brother—and generally acts interested in others by asking questions and listening to what they say. Children like Tina, who are sensitive to what others feel and have the confidence to reach out to them, are, not surprisingly, popular with their peers, teachers, and other adults alike.

People skills are more than just a set of rules for children to follow. Instead, they depend on attitude and judgment. Kids can lack people skills just as some adults do, and they often need help to learn them and reminders to use them.

Sizing up a situation

To fit in with others and get along in social situations, children need to be able to figure out what behavior is appropriate for different people and occasions. As we all know, what kids' friends expect from them isn't necessarily the same as what adults expect. Seven-year-old Dylan, for example, recently won a who-could-belch-the-loudest contest during recess, delighting all his friends. But he is savvy enough *not* to show off his winning belch during choir practice at his church, even if he's tempted to. Rebecca likes seeing how far she can spit watermelon seeds in her backyard when she's horsing around with her two older brothers. But when her friend's mom served watermelon for dessert at the dinner table, Rebecca carefully removed each seed from her mouth and placed it on the edge of her plate.

If what's appropriate isn't clear-cut, kids may need hints in advance from parents. And sometimes, when they learn by trial and error and wind up embarrassed, they need our sympathy.

Being able to enter a group

We've all witnessed the painful scene of a child standing forlornly outside a group, watching with longing as the other kids play kickball or just hang out together, telling jokes and talking. Whether kids are five or nine or thirteen, if they don't grasp the subtle nuances of how to enter and be accepted by a group of classmates, they have a hard time making friends, especially in the difficult preteen years.

Experts say there are several steps to entering a group so kids won't be rebuffed. The main thing is going slow and watching carefully on the sidelines until kids understand what's going on. Just standing there for a while, without talking, lets others become comfortable with a child's presence. Then he or she can do or say something tentative to show they've been watching.

What Social Skills Do Kids Need?

DID YOU KNOW ?

◆ Thomas Jefferson had a different idea of the essential social skills. In a letter written in 1783 to his daughter Martha at school in Philadelphia, he listed the skills he expected her to practice each day and for how long:

"From eight to ten, practise music, from ten to one dance one day and draw another, from three to four read French, from four to five exercise yourself in music, from five until bedtime, read English and write."

A boy who wants to join a kickball game might start running around at the edge of the group. One essential for kids is waiting until people seem to accept their presence completely before offering an opinion or grabbing the ball. Being bossy or critical is bad manners and will usually lead to rejection.

Choosing the right group to approach is important, too. A middle-school girl trying to edge into a cluster of popular girls may be rejected no matter what she does. Whatever their age, kids are likely to have better luck with a group of four or more whose interests are similar to their own, or which has especially friendly kids.

Putting people at ease

We all know adults that somehow manage to make us feel comfortable and at ease when we're around them. Some children, like Tina, have this ability, too. With a little prompting from parents, kids can begin to develop this skill, but it's easier for some kids than others. Knowing how to strike up a conversation and then keep it going (see pages 82-83), as well as having conversational skills like letting another person finish talking before *you* start talking, are part of it. Another is appearing friendly and interested in other people. Kids who look down at their feet instead of at another child, for example, appear unfriendly and ill at ease themselves.

These skills are especially important to self-conscious eleven- to thirteen-year-olds and shy children.

Giving compliments

It's a fact: complimenting a classmate on a new haircut, a baseball buddy on his pitching skill, or a friend's mom on her lasagne will make each one feel terrific. Researchers have found that the children who pay compliments most often get along better with other kids. Though many children feel shy about praising others, this is another skill parents can help them develop. One way is by pointing out how much *you* appreciate it when your children say things like "Your dress is pretty, Mom." If they report that a friend is a whiz at computer games, suggest, "Why don't you tell him? People like to hear things like that."

Reading and giving social cues

We let people know how we feel about them and learn how they feel about us by using and interpreting certain accepted social cues. Jimmy knows his friend Patrick is glad to see him because Patrick smiles and waves as Jimmy rides his bike up the walk. When Mona's teacher, Mrs. Sicher, puts her hands on her hips, folds her mouth into a straight line, and then calls out "Mona!" in a stern tone, Mona thinks, "Uh-oh, Mrs. Sicher doesn't like what I'm doing."

ADVICE FROM KIDS

How do you join a group of classmates at recess?

○ "If the kids are in your class, ask them about the homework," offers Sarah, 7.

○ "Stand so you can hear what they're saying, then say something about what they're talking about," advises Sebastian, 10.

○ "If you know one person in the group, stand next to her and say hi," says Andrea, 13.

Some children readily pick up on what another person's tone of voice, facial expression, gestures, and even posture convey; other kids just don't seem to get these forms of nonverbal communication and need help learning how to interpret them. They may think a sad expression is really an angry one or greet friends with a grumpy frown instead of a welcoming smile, or do things that actually turn others off, like standing too close and talking too loudly or in a monotone.

Resolving conflicts

Teachers who have taught elementary school for many years agree that a key ingredient for a child's social success is knowing how to disagree politely without losing control or showing belligerence toward the other person. In fact, they've discovered that the children who can keep their cool during disagreements and communicate without hostility often become the leaders in their schools: they are the captains of sports teams, the student government representatives, and the editors of the school newspaper. ❑

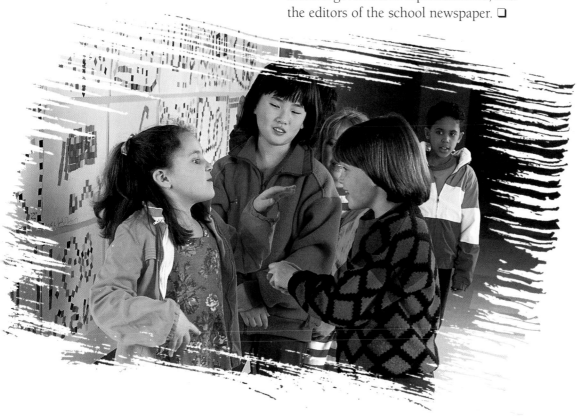

Can Kids Learn Tact?

One Christmas when my son was six he received a Barney stuffed animal, which, in his opinion, was the height of insult. After all, he was in the first grade! The gift was from my well-meaning cousin who was childless and obviously unaware of the nuances of age-appropriate gifts. My son, having been nagged into basic good manners by yours truly, managed to mutter, "Thank you," in the most sullen tone I'd ever heard. When my cousin asked worriedly whether he really liked the gift, my son looked up, rather cheered that he had been asked, and said, "No, I hate Barney." Dead silence from all of us while I tried to think of what to say. Then my son brightened and patted my cousin's arm in an affectionate way, and said very nicely, "But don't worry. We can give it to the Salvation Army."

Later, my cousin and I were able to chuckle over my son's lame attempt at tact. But I was also struck by how difficult it is for children to understand and act on this concept. As my son explained to me that night when I told him how his words made my cousin feel, "I'm sorry I hurt her feelings, Mom, but you always say not to tell a lie. What was I supposed to say?"

The difference between tact and a lie

It doesn't take long for kids to understand that although they *should* tell the truth,

▶ PARENT TIPS

How one parent helps tact along:

▶ Patricia, mother of 3 boys, says, "I try to let my kids know before a party if there's something unusual about a guest—if one of them is fat or bald, for example, or has a big beard, a scar, or a disability. That way the kids know what to expect and are less likely to blurt out some awful comment. I remind them it's not tactful to say anything that might embarrass someone, like asking why they don't have any hair."

there are times when telling the *complete* truth would make the other person feel bad. To help my son make the distinction in the case of the Barney gift, I asked him to think of other ways he could have responded. Together we came up with three possibilities that would have made my cousin feel much better than my son's original response:

- "I love stuffed animals!"
- "Dinosaurs are my favorite animals!"
- "Thanks for getting me a gift. I'm getting a little old for Barney, though."

By the time we finished brainstorming, my son was beginning to grasp the idea that being tactful is saying something careful so as not to hurt the other person's feelings. You can be fairly direct, but only if you show care and concern.

Plan in advance

Even older kids, who know better, may blurt out, "Mom, Mr. Allen's wig is slipping!" in a whisper loud enough to be overheard. In addition to reminding kids not to make personal remarks, it also helps to appeal to their sense of empathy with how-would-you-feel questions. One mom encourages her children to anticipate what to say in tricky situations, as in:

- When your sister asks, "Do you like my new haircut?" you could say, "It must feel good to have shorter hair."
- When your grandmother serves you the poached salmon she's prepared and asks, "Do you like it?" you could say "No offense, Grandma, but is it okay if I just eat your yummy mashed potatoes!"

Watch how others use tact

Since the Barney incident, my son and I have been on tact alert, another way I've found to teach the concept. We watch for successful tactful comments on television shows and at family gatherings, and my son looks for them when he's playing with friends. He reports that his soccer coach always says, "Good effort" when a player misses a goal, and I report that our neighbor said she liked the size of our new glass coffee table even though I know the style is not to her taste.

This has become something of a game, and I've found the more we point out instances of tact, the more my son is aware of how being tactful is an important aspect of kindness to others.

Those embarrassing moments

In spite of all your best efforts, accept that your children will occasionally embarrass you by a brutally frank comment and stubbornly stick to the subject even when you attempt to curtail it. Your best bet is to exit the scene as quickly as possible, apologizing if necessary, and tell your child, "Remember what I said about making personal remarks? We'll talk about this in private." ❑

ADVICE FROM KIDS

What do you say to be tactful?

- "I laughed at a joke my uncle told even though he already told the same joke to me the last time I saw him," reports Brianna, 7.

- "When my grandmother gave me underwear for my birthday, I said, 'I really need underwear,' even though it was the last thing I wanted as a present," says Ryan, 9.

- "I told my friend's mom I wasn't very hungry when she offered me some tofu at dinner," offers Melissa, 13.

Which Social Rules Are Still Important?

To many parents, this question is the big one. These days it's frequently difficult to figure out which rules for children are necessary and which have fallen by the wayside. No one still thinks boys should bow and girls curtsy, but should they call our friends by their first names or still use Mr. and Mrs.? Are thank-you notes mandatory for every gift received? Should a child stand up when an older person comes into the room? What about offering his or her seat on the bus to someone who needs it? Then there's the question of whether you ought to bow to the contemporary world and allow your child to begin every sentence with the word "Yo!" or wear his beloved Mets hat at the Thanksgiving dinner table.

These questions are easier to answer when we base our manners teaching on two important tenets of etiquette—kindness and respect—instead of formal rules.

Social rules rooted in kindness still apply

Most parents would agree with Robin's mom. She's more concerned about whether her twelve-year-old son helps a neighbor with his garden or a blind person cross the mall thoroughfare than whether he recognizes the difference between a demitasse spoon and a dessert spoon. Other still essential social rules are the ones designed to prevent hurt feelings, like banning name-calling and insulting remarks. Beatrice's mom mails kindergarten party invitations because it's kinder than handing them out in school where an uninvited child might feel rejected.

At the dinner table we want our child to offer the bread to the person sitting next to him first and refrain from pronouncing the food yucky because these are kind things to do and thus more important than following the formal rule of passing food to the left instead of the right (see pages 48-51).

We teach kids to RSVP to an invitation as soon as possible because it will help the hostess with party plans. And yes, thank-you notes to people who have given a gift or provided a special outing or treat are mandatory because they make people feel appreciated (see pages 54-55). At the heart of these kind manners is the idea that children are learning to think beyond themselves and consider others.

Respect is always a social rule

One way our kids show respect to adults is by the way they address them, and today that's a complicated issue. Although I remember referring to all my parents' friends as Mr. or Mrs., for example, my own close friends insist that my children refer to them by their first names. Many of us live in areas where both forms of address prevail. So, like many parents, I've solved the problem by telling my children to call adults by Mr. or Mrs. or their title, as in Doctor Smith or Reverend Brown, until or unless they request otherwise. Many experts suggest that kids should save "yo" and other "in" slang forms of address for friends and show respect by not using them with adults.

At the Hartmans' house, as in many others, treating older people with respect is also still a manners priority. Jan, age six, Barbara, age ten, and Kevin, age twelve, cheerfully (usually) defer to their grandpa's choice of TV program, hold the door for him, and are willing to listen to the war stories he likes to tell over and over. On the other hand, they don't stand up when he or other adults walk into the room. Many parents don't expect their kids to do this, but be aware that some do because it makes adults feel welcomed and respected.

Wearing appropriate clothes is another mark of respect to others that still holds (see pages 66-67). If Mike wears a T-shirt full of holes and a dirty baseball cap to a family party at Aunt Betty's house, it conveys that Mark—and his parents—don't think the occasion or his aunt is worth dressing up for. The rules for what children should wear to school today are less clear. But some schools are now instituting uniforms precisely because they believe it helps kids be more respectful to teachers and one another. ❑

Why Do Some Schools Teach Manners?

Believe it or not, years ago etiquette was a formally taught subject, part of the curriculum in both public and private schools. What was taught depended upon the status of the school. Public schools focused on correct behavior toward "your betters"; private schools held social dancing classes that prepared girls and boys for upcoming cotillions and balls. As our society became more and more informal, though, very few schools took the time to teach children etiquette.

Now manners classes in schools are coming back. The main reason? Parents, teachers, and principals alike are concerned about the *lack* of manners that children regularly display on the playground, on the playing field, in the cafeteria, and in the classroom. Teachers and researchers report that children today are not only ruder to one another, they also are ruder and especially more disrespectful to teachers, coaches, and other school personnel.

Should schools teach manners?

We tend to think of school as a place where kids learn academic subjects—reading, writing, and math—but it's also where they learn to get along with other children as well as those in authority. The truth is, kids who don't know how to ask a teacher for help, follow instructions when asked, or get the teacher's attention politely are at a great disadvantage. If students lack social skills, they may have trouble making friends and, as a result be too unhappy to concentrate on schoolwork. A school that doesn't insist kids treat one another with kindness and respect may be a place where bullying and mean behavior flourishes.

Ways schools teach manners

Many schools incorporate informal lessons on manners when the need arises. A teacher at one middle school instituted weekly manners sessions on how to disagree, compliment, and be polite to others because she observed several children bragging and being rude during cooperative math projects. Another, appalled by the way students interrupted each other—and him—during discussions in English class, handed out a manners list of how to participate in a class discussion. And when a social studies teacher introduced a unit on manners in early America, he was surprised that the thirteen-year-olds in his class were most concerned about and wanted to discuss at length what manners were appropriate when dealing with the opposite sex today.

Some school districts, often at the suggestion of the PTA, are bringing independent children's etiquette programs into their schools. A Cincinnati-based program, AT EASE, INC., has taught manners to over eighty thousand children in public and private schools, camps,

and youth organizations.

In teaching the art of conversation to one third grade, the director of the program discovered students had no idea that when people are gathered together, they should act interested in the other people by asking polite questions.

In the lunchroom

Have you visited a school lunchroom lately? Most parents are appalled by what they see and hear—yelling, food fights, kids shoveling food into their mouths and leaving a mess on the tables, and more. The decline in kids' table manners inspired Kevin Kile, the principal of Royerton Elementary School in Muncie, Indiana, to start "Lunch at the Ritz," a special lunchtime manners class run by parent volunteers. The class is a reward for the students who have been on their best behavior in the cafeteria—meaning keeping voices down and eating with proper utensils. Tablecloths and matching napkins, flowers, and wineglasses filled with milk grace each table at the "Ritz," waiters show kids to reserved seats, and kids wear their best clothes and delight in feeling grown-up. Parents have noticed a carryover in improved table manners at home, too.

Gaining self-confidence

Another reason schools are adding manners to their curriculum is because teachers believe that knowing the right way to behave makes kids more confident and boosts their self-esteem in ways that have an impact on their schoolwork. Bob Maul, who teaches manners and ethics in several suburban Ohio elementary schools, reports that kids who take his course see themselves as "winners instead of losers." ❑

DID YOU KNOW ?

◆ Basic manners at schools in Japan are more formal than in the United States. Even preschoolers bow from the waist when greeting classmates or saying goodbye to them.

◆ Your child's school can order AT EASE's *Manners-In-A-Flash*, sets of flash cards in several categories including 1 on school manners. This one covers such topics as cafeteria and library manners and how to greet a teacher (see page 95).

Is It Ever Too Late To Start Teaching Manners?

Not really, but if you wait until your kids are teenagers to teach manners, good luck, because you'll probably have a pretty hard time! Introducing a few basics before the age of seven or eight and building on these over the next several years makes your task easier, say manners experts and parents with experience, such as my friend Nancy. She didn't start teaching her twin boys manners in a serious way until they were nine—because she gave birth to girl twins when the boys were four! Manners training for all of them started five years later.

How starting earlier helps

At five years of age, Nancy found, her daughters, like most kids, were still at the eager-to-please stage and took pride in keeping napkins on laps, among other things. Over the next few years they mastered table manners at a faster pace than their brothers because of this earlier foundation in doing the right thing. By seven they had developed some empathy for others and knew unkind remarks hurt. And by nine, as new experiences came along, they were able to build on what they already knew. Practice makes perfect. If children begin learning manners at ages five, six, or seven, they'll be second nature (we hope) by the time kids are teenagers.

If your kids are preteens

If you've waited until your child is eleven or twelve, there's still hope. As children get older, they are often motivated to learn manners because they don't want to be embarrassed—they want to know how to act at a party or on a first date.

Nancy's boys, for example, were anxious to learn proper behavior when they received invitations to a friend's bar mitzvah. They wanted to look cool at the party afterward, which would include a deejay, elaborate buffet dinner, and after-dinner speeches. Nancy was able to coach two very cooperative sons in social rules like how to behave inside a synagogue, how to ask a girl to dance, and how to get food from a buffet table, and managed to slip in a few hints on table manners, too. ❏

▶ PARENT TIPS

What manners did you learn early that you use without thinking?

▶ "We always had to stand whenever an adult came into a classroom at the Catholic elementary school I attended. To this day, I automatically rise whenever any adult enters a room," says Rick, father of 2.

▶ "My mother was a stickler on elaborate table manners, and my chore was setting the table. I remember the details so well I could set the Queen of England's table," reports Margaret, mother of 3.

▶ "Having to compose thank-you notes in my mother's bedroom, using her lavender stationery, and redoing them until I got her okay was torture. But today I don't put off writing them!" says Rose, mother of 2.

WHAT TO DO
The Best Advice

How To Teach Your Child Manners

Two weeks before her mother-in-law's sixtieth birthday party at an elegant French restaurant in Boston, Alecia panicked and decided she'd better improve the table manners of her seven-year-old daughter, Madeline, and five-year-old son, Ben. At the first lesson, Alecia tried to teach them to put napkins on their laps, use outside forks for salad and big spoons for soup, cut meat into small pieces, and keep bread on the bread plate and elbows off the table. The class, reports Alecia, was not a success. She grew impatient, Madeline left the dining room in tears, and Ben announced grumpily that he didn't want to go to the party, anyway.

Like Alecia, many of us remember the importance of manners only when we are forced by circumstance to teach them to our children. Then we institute a quick crash course and try to teach five or six elaborate rules at one time to a child who may be too young to learn them properly. Guess what? It won't work. When teaching our kids manners, we first have to recognize that it takes time, patience, a sense of humor, and a systematic approach.

Make a realistic plan

When Alecia calmed down, she realized that getting Madeline and Ben to sit through even a thirty-minute meal would be an accomplishment and that she could not turn them into Little Miss and Mr. Perfect Manners by the night of the party. She could, however, teach them a few basic skills over the next two weeks. After several "sitting still" dinners with their parents instead of their usual early dinner in the kitchen, Madeline and Ben learned to wait until the hostess—in this case, Mommy—sat down before they lunged for any food. By the night of the party they even put napkins on their laps and used forks—most of the time.

Before you start teaching manners, decide on one or two areas to tackle first. Maria, for example, realized her nine-year-old son's usual way of answering the phone was a rude "Yeah?" and that she cringed every time he picked up the receiver before she could get there. She started with the telephone. If you can barely endure sitting across the dinner table because your son talks with food in his mouth or your daughter slurps spaghetti through her teeth, then make table manners your first priority. The main things to remember: start with a few

▶ PARENT TIPS

▶ Kathy, mother of a 6- and an 8-year-old, says, "We realized our kids weren't getting enough practice in manners, so we've instituted several regular family rituals. One is a regular movie night at home when we pretend we're at a theater and another is a special once a week dinner out."

simple changes, work on these until kids usually incorporate them, and only then begin teaching other skills.

Set an example

Sometimes the hardest part about teaching manners is being a role model for your child. As most parents learn the hard way, "Do as I say, not as I do" simply does not work. If you want your kids to eat at the table and not standing at the counter, you have to do that, too—and resist the temptation to finish the leftover coleslaw at the kitchen sink. The more you say please and thank you to your children, the more likely they are to use these words themselves. And if you are embarrassed by the intrusive and nosy questions your child asks her neighborhood playmates, then be sure she doesn't overhear you asking your next-door neighbor, "Gee Marie, how many times has that woman down the street been divorced, anyway?"

It's true that our kids are often oblivious to the example we're setting—especially when we want them to notice something positive—so it helps to provide commentary, as in "I'm going to call Mrs. Telik to thank her for her help as soon as I get home!" or "I held the door for the man with the cane because it's so heavy."

Teach kids what to do

As adults, we often forget that our kids don't automatically know how to sit in a polite way at the dinner table or that they should say hello to the dad who's driving them to hockey practice. In order to teach manners, we have to demonstrate what we want our kids to do in a very clear, direct way, as in "This is the way you put your fork and knife on the plate when you clear your place" or "When Daddy's friend from the office, Mr. Elkins, comes for dinner, look him in the eye like this, then shake hands and say hello." Be very specific about expectations: "Hold your fork like this." "Say, 'please pass the peas,' instead of reaching." "If you dial a wrong number by mistake, apologize." Teaching do's instead of don'ts is usually more effective.

Give reasons for being polite

Many kids whine, "Why do I hafta be polite?" In order to make manners stick, kids need to hear both the general rule of thinking about others and the logic behind a specific rule.

Suzanne, for example, frequently tells her children, "I want people to like you. When you're polite, people are happy to see you and *do* like you." This is a persuasive reason to children at any age. Some parents ask their kids how-would-you-feel-if questions ("How would you feel if someone pushed in front of you in line?")

and remind them that manners are a way of treating others with the thoughtfulness they like to receive, too.

But kids remember rules better when they also hear a specific reason, as in "If you talk during the movie, other people can't hear the actors" or "If you don't take a message, I don't know who to call back."

Kids need prompting

As we all know, when your child is about to leave a party or someone else's house, it never hurts to whisper, "Did you remember to thank Kyla and her mom?"

Regular prompting about all manners is essential for kids, even older ones. But how you do it makes a difference. Gently correcting your child privately or using a whisper or special signal if you're in public won't embarrass him or her. Reminding kids of a rule ("It's polite to eat birthday cake with a fork") always works better than making a negative comment ("You're eating that cake like a slob").

You don't always have to use words to remind kids, either: I stand at the refrigerator, firmly holding the glass of lemonade while my son's arm is outstretched until it dawns on him to say, "Thanks, Mom."

Praise counts, too

Have you ever noticed how a child beams after his or her good behavior is acknowledged? Reinforce the manners you want

ASK THE EXPERTS

• **Paula Person, director of The Children's Spoon™, an etiquette program based in Winnetka, Illinois, recommends playing games and singing songs to reinforce social manners in young children.**

by lavishing praise for even the smallest improvement. "Emma, since you asked so politely, I'll give you the chocolate cookies you want" is a response that kids remember, as is "I liked the way you opened the door for your Aunt Ella. That just shows how grown-up you are!" Louise, mother of two girls, writes notes after a special party telling her daughters that she was proud of the way they behaved and sticks the notes on their doors.

What *doesn't* work is comparing. Comments like "Why can't you be as polite as your sister?" or "Your friend Matt certainly has better table manners than you do!" are guaranteed to create jealousy and resentment instead of improving manners.

Practice makes perfect

As in just about everything children learn, practice is essential. Alecia's children, for example, rarely ate dinner with their parents, so they'd had very little practice with correct table manners. Experts such as Sandra Loughran, a psychologist and director of a private elementary school on Long Island, explain that practicing before a certain situation is also important. She says, "If you're having company on Saturday, play some games beforehand. Have your daughter open the door and greet you as the pretend guest. Practicing ahead of time lowers your child's anxiety as well as yours." (See pages 68-69.)

Be consistent

"Never let it slide" is my friend Carol's rule of thumb. Her eleven-year-old daughter is one of the most well-mannered children I've ever met. Consistency, insists Carol, makes the difference, and experts agree. Of course, this is a goal that few can sustain all the time—we permit lapses, especially on occasions like take-out pizza night.

But when we stand firm in the face of resistance to manners, whether from a five-year-old or a thirteen-year-old, we let kids know manners matter. After all, if they *don't* have to use good manners on a daily basis, they are quick to assume that politeness probably isn't that essential.

Be patient

Ages five through ten are the prime years for teaching basic manners. Experts agree, though, that we'll be more successful if we match our expectations with the appropriate age. By the end of kindergarten, for example, kids can master key words like "please" and "thank you," but expecting them to use the correct fork is unrealistic.

Keep in mind that although a child has learned to come to the table with a clean face and hands at age six, that doesn't mean you won't still be reminding him or her occasionally at age twelve. Age guidelines (see pages 87-90) don't take into account an important fact—that teaching manners is a long-term project. ❑

· · · · · · · · · · · · · · · · · ·

DID YOU KNOW ?

◆ Children's manners are becoming more and more important to adults. In a 1991 survey conducted by the Roper-Starch Worldwide marketing firm, 49% of Americans expressed the view that "good manners and politeness are especially important qualities to teach children." In the 1995 survey, that figure rose to 59%.

· · · · · · · · · · · · · · · · · ·

The Essential Words For Kids To Learn

Whenever twelve-year-old Sabrina has to use the town library for a school project, the reference librarian is happy to help her hunt for needed books, guide her through using the copy machine, and even look up related articles on the InfoTrac.

At the local record store, the busy clerk was willing to check in the stockroom for the latest hot CD when ten-year-old Jessica requested it, so she was able to buy it before any of her friends.

The barber offers six-year-old Brian a lollipop whenever he gets a haircut—and always says, "Take an extra one for later."

How do these children manage to get what they want? Why are they thought of by everyone as nice kids? You can probably guess the answer. Because they consistently use the key words and phrases of politeness—"please," "thank you," "excuse me," and "may I?"

If we instill these phrases in our children—generally by using them ourselves when we talk to others and by frequent reminders—they will eventually use them automatically. And as a result, our kids will find their world a friendlier, kinder place.

"Please"

This is the single most important word kids need to know, one that many, like Sabrina, learn as early as two or three years of age. Sabrina's mom would say, "What's the magic word?" when Sabrina asked for something, and with a little smile she would reply, "Pweeze?"

Children need lots of assistance in their daily lives, and using please before or after requests for help gets them quicker and much more enthusiastic responses from just about everyone: "I need another pencil, please" to the teacher; "Mom, more juice, please" at the dinner table; and "Please lower the boom box—my parents will freak!" with friends.

Although other adults may not pay much attention to the word when *we* say it, you can bet that *not* hearing please from a child is definitely noticed.

"Thank you"

This should be your children's response whenever someone does something for them or gives them something, no matter how small. That means when they're handed an ice-cream cone or a lollipop, as Brian was, when an adult drives them home, and when they're invited to a party. It can easily be combined with please, as in "Please pass the ketchup, Dad. Thanks." It can end a telephone conversation, as in "Thanks for calling." And when someone asks your child, "How are you?" the answer can be "Fine, thanks."

Thanking someone can be a polite way to say no, too. If your son, for example, doesn't want to play at Billy's house but doesn't want to hurt his feelings, teach him to say nicely, "I can't come over today, but thanks for asking me."

Reinforce thanking, as Brian's mom does, by reminding kids of how good their words of appreciation make someone feel.

Of course, the reverse of this is responding when people thank *you*. Some kids just stand there blankly. But what they should say is a cheerful, "You're welcome."

"Excuse me" or "Sorry"

"Excuse me" or "sorry" should be used whenever a child bumps into someone, has to apologize, or needs to interrupt. These words go a long way toward making amends when children spill milk at home or push a friend accidentally on the playground. A simple "Oops, sorry!" when kids play too rough with grandparents or a little sister or brother can show sensitivity and consideration.

When kids approach any adult for help, they will find they get friendlier, more thorough attention if they say, "Excuse me. Could you please help me with . . .?" as Jessica did with the store clerk. Sometimes kids do need to interrupt an adult conversation, and if they say, "Sorry for interrupting, but . . .," the interruption will seem far less intrusive than "Mom, I need . . ."

When your son or daughter does something wrong, the word "sorry" works wonders in most situations. And saying "excuse me," not wild giggles, is the polite way to react if you burp or pass gas, a fact that you may need to repeat many, many times until your child is a teenager.

"May I?"

As an English teacher I admit I prefer "May I?" to "Can I?" but the truth is, either one is perfectly acceptable. The point is that a child needs to learn to *ask* for something instead of *demanding* it. "I want more popcorn," or worse, "More popcorn!" should be rephrased, "May I have more popcorn, please?" "It's my turn on the computer," should be "Could I please have my turn on the computer now?"

Adults can set a good example with this one by asking, "Could I hear you practice your piano lessons?" instead of simply ordering, "Time to practice!" ❏

▶ PARENT TIPS

How to remember to say please and thank you:

▶ "In our family, we make remembering these words a game. Whoever forgets a please or thank you has to give up a quarter, which goes in a jar on the kitchen counter. It's usually my husband who forgets, and the kids love correcting him!" offers Marcie, mother of a boy and a girl.

▶ "I don't honor requests that don't end with a please. Now my kids know that if I respond with dead silence and a blank stare, it means they forgot the please," says Aphelia, mother of 2 girls.

About Meeting & Greeting

One of the most important skills we can teach our kids is the art of meeting new people and greeting those they already know. Many parents today, like Lenny's dad, complain that children often act as though adults are invisible. "I think children are being rude if they don't at least say, 'Hi!' pleasantly when they get in your car or walk into your living room," he says. Most adults feel the same way. In truth, everyone likes to be acknowledged, from a visiting aunt to your child's friend who lives down the street.

The main reasons kids simply grunt something unintelligible or ignore people are that they feel shy and awkward and sometimes aren't sure what to do. But greeting people politely is the first step in getting to know someone new and in treating those you do know with respect. Children need this skill on the playground and with adults as they grow up. Keep in mind, though, that naturally outgoing kids learn to greet people and introduce themselves more easily and at earlier ages than shy, timid ones do.

Meeting and greeting adults

Giving children a standard routine for what to do and say when they meet someone is the best way to help them get over feelings of shyness or awkwardness and appear confident. When Lenny was six, he and his dad played a game—his dad pretended to be different, sometimes silly, people for Lenny to greet. Here are the basic steps for meeting someone new or greeting your next-door neighbor, the scout leader, or your mom's best friend:

- Smile and look the person in the eye. (Some parents also insist their children stand up.)
- Shake hands.
- Say hello and if possible, the person's name—"Hello, Mrs. Johnson"—in a voice loud enough for the person to hear.

Of course, you need to make sure you *introduce* Mrs. Johnson to your child to prompt him or her to *use* this routine with someone new. Unfortunately, parents sometimes forget this. Keep the introductions simple: "Dorothy, this is my son, Alex. Alex, this is Mrs. Johnson."

Not all parents today belong to the stand-when-an-adult-comes-into-the-room

▶ PARENT TIPS

How to practice making introductions:

▶ "I insist my son introduce his friends to me—even if he's casually chatting to an acquaintance on the driveway," reports Sarah, mother of 2.

▶ "It's a family rule that we introduce whoever enters our house to the family. When I host my bridge club or a meeting, I introduce my daughters to everyone, so they don't act shy anymore," says Barbara, mother of 2.

school as I do. But adults *appreciate* this form of respect and many, including authorities your child will encounter over the years, such as principals, expect it. If you want to encourage your kids to develop this habit, however, start before they enter middle school.

Meeting new kids

Obviously, seven-year-old Jacob doesn't need to shake hands when he meets a new second grader on the playground. He does, however, need to say *something* friendly and welcoming. Jacob's mom suggested he go up to the new kid, say, "Hi, I'm Jacob. What's

your name?" and ask a question or two, such as "Where are you from?" or "Do you walk home or take the bus?" This method works just as well when kids are in their preteens, though the questions will be more along the lines of "What kind of music do you like?" or "What sport do you play?"

Making introductions

First, it's not unreasonable to insist that your kids introduce their friends to you. A next step is teaching them to introduce a friend to another friend. Outgoing kids can even learn to say, "Hi, I'm Ellen," if nobody else introduces them.

We all know adults who avoid introductions because they're not sure whom to introduce first. But basic introductions are easy. "Billy, this is Ryan. Ryan, this is Billy" is just fine. As a child gets older he can learn to introduce the adult to the younger person first, as in "Mom, this is Don. Don, this is my mother, Mrs. Nelson."

After we're introduced to someone, there is often an awful pause when neither knows what to say next. This is common when kids are preteens, too, so suggest a line kids can add to get a conversation rolling, as in "Vic's dad is our baseball coach." ❏

AGE FACTOR

❖ A 5-year-old might have trouble knowing what to say when meeting a new person, but an 8-year-old should do fine with this.

❖ A 9-year-old should be able to make simple introductions with a little prompting.

❖ A 13-year-old should know how to introduce people to each other with no prompting and be able to do this smoothly.

About Table Manners & Eating Out

For many parents, the number one manners concern is their children's table manners. If parents haven't stressed table manners much, they wonder what they should teach and when. If they've already introduced the basics, they ask themselves, as Jason's mom did, "Why do I constantly have to remind Jason to use his napkin? Why can't he remember to eat with his mouth closed?" In truth, no one enjoys sitting across the table from a child who is chewing a large piece of meat and at the same time telling a new joke he heard during recess. Nor is it pleasant to hear "Gimme the hot dogs" or "This fish looks yucky."

Actually, teaching table manners is the biggest manners challenge for parents. For one thing, there seem to be so many rules to convey. For another, they're not just based on simple kindness and courtesy, but on more formal— and arbitrary—rules and traditions, many from the Middle Ages.

Why kids lack table manners

One of the main reasons children's table manners are on a decline, say experts, is that so few families today eat a sit-down dinner together regularly. In fact, studies show that few do this more than twice a week! Yet all experts agree that the easiest and most effective way to teach children table manners is to eat dinner with them on a daily basis. Jason's mom,

for example, found it not only resulted in better manners, but also helped her children learn punctuality, conversation skills, and respect for others.

Twelve basic table rules

The first step in tackling your kids' table manners is deciding what to teach. I've gleaned the following essentials from several children's etiquette experts, who advise parents to start with the first one or two in each category, focus on those until they seem established, then add more.

Though children in elementary school *should* know these basics, don't expect kids to use them all the time. Kids frequently relax and forget and regress at home, but behave perfectly when at a friend's house.

Before eating:

- Come to the table with washed hands and clean face. Don't wear a hat, even your favorite baseball cap.
- Take a seat, place napkin and hands on lap, and *wait* for the hostess—usually Mom—to sit down and begin serving or eating *before* you start yourself.
- When passed a bowl of food, put a spoonful on your plate, then pass the bowl to the person next to you. If you want the French fries, ask, "Please pass the French fries." Don't grab or reach.

While eating:

- Use utensils—don't eat with your fingers. Hold your fork like a pencil and when cutting food, press down on the back of the fork and the knife with your index finger.
- Chew with your mouth closed and don't talk with your mouth open. Taking small bites makes this easier.
- Keep your elbows off the table and your free hand in your lap.
- Break off a small piece of bread (not a tiny crumb) and butter one piece at a time, holding it over the plate.
- If you must cough or sneeze, turn your head to the side and cover your mouth with your napkin.
- Remove an olive pit or piece of gristle by covering your mouth, releasing the item into your cupped hand, and placing it unobtrusively onto your plate.
- If you need to excuse yourself for a moment, leave your napkin on the chair.

When you're finished:

- Place the knife and fork sideways on your plate; blot your lips with your napkin, then place the napkin to the right of your plate.
- Ask, "May I please be excused?" before leaving the table.

These basic rules are the same whether your kids are eating at home, at a friend's house, or in a restaurant. They don't include such obvious things as staying seated or not playing with food. But a few problem situations regularly crop up when eating out.

ADVICE FROM KIDS

○ "My mom tried to lecture me about table manners stuff, but I didn't really learn until we started having dinner together in the dining room twice a week," says Joshua, 8.

○ "I remember where the silverware goes by the amount of letters: 'knife' and 'spoon' and 'glass' have 5 letters, they go on the 'right,' which also has 5 letters. 'Fork' and 'dish'—for bread dish—goes on the 'left,' which all have 4 letters," declares Samantha, 10.

"That looks yucky!"

We've all been at a meal—maybe at a good friend's house—where our kids were offered food that they dislike, and we cringed when they said forthrightly, "That looks yucky" or "I hate fish." Experts would agree with Billy's dad, who told his son, "When Grandma brings out a dish with great fanfare and announces, 'Here it is, Billy, Grandma's special recipe of liver and onions!' you have to be polite and take at least a tiny portion to try." I taught my children two pat phrases to use when they don't want a particular dish—"No thank you, I have so much on my plate now" and "Maybe later, thanks."

If the offending food is already on the plate, tell your children to simply ignore it rather than ask for it to be removed, even if it is touching the mashed potatoes!

Different family traditions

Children often assume that every family behaves the way theirs does, but traditions vary. The Sullivans, for example, always recite a grace together before eating. The MacAllisters observe a moment of silence, bow their heads, and hold hands. The Romano family waits for Mrs. Romano to say, "Please start, everyone." Children need to know that they should follow the lead of the adults whose home they're visiting, and bow their heads as a sign of respect if a prayer is said.

No changing seats

This problem occurs at family holiday gatherings. Your child, especially a preteen, complains because he's seated next to ninety-year-old Aunt Tanya instead of his favorite cousin. But once seated, your child shouldn't request a change. It's only for a meal, and this is an opportunity for him to make his aunt feel good.

The table setting

Table manners include knowing where plates, glasses, and utensils go on the table. Start by teaching this basic table setting:
○ Knife, turned inward, to the right of the plate, the teaspoon to its right. A soup spoon goes to the teaspoon's right.
○ Fork on the left; salad fork to its left if salad is served before the main dish, to its right if served after the main dish; dessert fork above the plate with a spoon.
○ Glass above the knife.
○ Bread plate above the fork.
○ Napkins can go anywhere, as long as they are neat and attractive.

Explain to older kids that you usually use the silverware farthest from your plate first, then work your way in.

What to do about restaurants

A word of warning: don't expect kids to know how to behave in restaurants (other than fast-food joints) if they hardly ever go to one! To insure their good behavior, prepare them in advance. Remember, they don't know many of the things you take for granted. For example, explain what type of restaurant you are going to and what it looks like, and be sure to describe probable food choices. This will help kids behave better once they're there.

If you can, and especially with younger children, go early, before the bulk of adult diners arrive, rather than later in the evening. Not only will service be faster and more attentive, but kids also have a chance to get used to the space before it becomes crowded. Also remember that when kids order for themselves—"May I please have the children's chicken nuggets?"—they feel more grown-up and generally behave better. At a fancy restaurant, younger children love to visit the bathroom, and this is a good way to pass the time while waiting for the food you've ordered to arrive.

Pick an appropriate restaurant

This may sound obvious but . . . If your children are under the age of eight, choose informal restaurants that welcome young children, offer food your children like, and get the food you've ordered on the table fairly quickly. We've always found diners, Chinese and Italian restaurants, and restaurants with an outdoor café to be good bets. Older kids can handle a more formal place if dinner doesn't take too much more than an hour. Interesting decor is also a big plus.

Special restaurant tips

We often forget that our children take their cues directly from us. If we treat servers and busboys politely, so will they. But if we don't, they won't. Here are some other tips:

◦ Keep children from playing with items on the table such as sugar bowls, pepper mills, salt shakers, and condiments by instituting a "hands off" rule and bringing paper and pencils to occupy them.

◦ Remind your kids not to stare at other diners and to talk quietly. Some parents tell kids to use "restaurant voices."

◦ Wandering around the restaurant or hiding under the table are big no-no's.

◦ Don't worry about details. Not annoying other diners is more important than holding a fork correctly.

◦ The right way to deal with straws is to remove the straw paper by tearing the top and pushing down the paper—*not* by banging the straw on the table.

◦ Bring a glass up to drink instead of leaving it on the table and bending down to slurp through the straw.

◦ If a napkin drops, don't dive to the floor to retrieve it. Instead, your child should raise his hand to get the server's attention (*not* snap his fingers) and ask, "May I please have another napkin?"

◦ Let the server remove plates. Many children think they're helping by handing their plates to the waitstaff, but in fact it is easier for them to remove dishes. ❏

AGE FACTOR

❖ Learning table manners is a cumulative process; at ages 5 and 6, good table manners may mean just remaining seated for the meal and using a fork.

❖ Eight- and 9-year-olds should be able to pass food to others, cut their own meat with a knife and fork, and butter a piece of bread, holding it over the plate.

❖ Twelve- and 13-year-olds should be able to make restaurant reservations and figure out a 15% tip.

About Telephone Manners

The phone rings as I'm getting out of the shower early on a Sunday morning. I manage to pick it up on the fourth ring, say hello, and a young voice asks abruptly, "Who's this?"

Annoyed, I reply, "Who is *this*?"

"I hafta talk to Alex right now," the caller demands. Reluctantly, wanting to be a nice mom, I find my son, hand over the portable phone, and later learn that the caller was his friend Joey.

This exchange, which probably sounds familiar even to parents with kids in middle school, reminds us that telephone manners are a skill many kids have not been taught. Yet the telephone is an important line to the outside world, and when we can't see the speaker's face, we form an impression based solely on his or her voice. The best way to help our kids learn telephone basics so they can communicate politely with that outside world is to teach them exactly what to say and how to say it.

Start with answering the phone

Many children grunt, "Yeah?" in a brusque way when they pick up the phone, which certainly sounds rude. Their friends probably won't care, but you never know who may be calling—it could be one of your business associates, the head of the PTA, or a bank officer responding to your request for a loan instead of your son's best friend.

My friend Eliza coached her eight-year-old daughter, Carol, to use the following polite phone-answering routine:

- Say "Hello" clearly in a pleasant way.
- Ask "Who's calling, please?"
- Greet the caller by name if it's someone you know, as in "Oh, hi, Mrs. Johnson."
- If a caller wants to speak to Mom or Dad or a sibling, say, "Please hold on. I'll tell her you're on the phone."
- If neither parent is home, explain, "My mom (or dad) can't come to the phone right now. May I take a message?" Kids should *not* admit a parent isn't home. (Even if there's no message, a child should write down the name and phone number.)
- Hang up immediately if the caller sounds weird or makes you uneasy.
- Say "Good-bye" before you hang up.

One thing that irritates me—and many other parents I know—is when my son

---

▶ **PARENT TIPS**

▶ "My kids kept forgetting to give me phone messages until I bought an official looking while-you-were-away message pad. I keep it by the phone with several pencils and now I get all my messages. The kids enjoy filling in the blanks with the caller's name, phone number, message, and time of call," says Darcy, mother of 2 girls.

▶ "When we got call waiting, we made a rule that if an adult calls for my wife or me while our kids are on the phone, they have to call their friend back unless they're getting help with homework," says Bob, father of 3.

or daughter rudely shouts, "Mom, it's for you!" at the top of his or her lungs. I try to insist my kids put the receiver down gently and come and get me or bring the cordless phone to me. Of course, they don't remember to do that very often!

Let kids know that if they pick up the extension and hear voices, that's the cue to hang up; eavesdropping is not polite.

Ending telephone conversations

Many kids can't think of a courteous way to get off the phone. In fact, younger kids sometimes need to be reminded to say good-bye! Ten-year-old Annabel feels trapped into staying on when she doesn't want to in order to be polite. Like her, kids are usually relieved to know it's okay to say, "It was nice talking to you, but I have to hang up now," during a pause. If a friend calls at a bad time, they can say: "We're having dinner. May I call you back later?" or "My dad needs to use the phone now, but he'll be through in ten minutes."

Making calls

My son's friend Joey, like many kids, didn't observe any of the rules for making calls politely:

- First of all, say who you are, as in "Hello, this is Joey." If you recognize the person who answers, say, for example, "Hi, Mrs. Leonard. This is Joey."
- Then ask nicely, "May I please speak to Alex?" If someone says he'll get your friend, reply, "Thank you."

Learning a few phrases to use if a friend isn't available helps younger kids. My son memorized these: "Could you please have him call me?" "When do you expect him back?" and "I'll call later."

- Don't call very early in the morning on weekends or late at night. In our house that means nine AM and ten PM.
- When your friend gets on the phone, say who you are again.
- Don't forget to say good-bye.

Many kids slam down the phone if they get a wrong number or say, "Who's this?" because they don't know what to do. They should ask, "Is this 555-6397?" and if it isn't, say, "I'm sorry."

Answering machines

These machines are a fixture in many households now, and some children feel more comfortable than others leaving a message on them. I've found it's best for kids to rely on simple preset phrases, as in "Hello, this is Brian Jones calling for Danny." Kids can add, "My number is 555-9687. Please call me back tomorrow morning" or "I'll be at soccer practice til three." If machines make your child nervous, tell him to hang up rather than leave a confusing mumble. By middle school many kids are articulate enough to leave a detailed message, but short is usually best. ❑

About Thank-You Notes

Getting children to write thank-you notes is not an easy task. Some parents just give up in the face of their kids' groans and wails. The objections that May, a mother of four, heard after Christmas last year are typical: "I don't know how to write a letter!" "The vest Aunt Liz made me is so-o-o ugly!" "There's a special TV program on now, and I'm missing it!" "I promise I'll do it tomorrow." May is adamant. Despite loud protests, her kids write thank-you notes for the presents they received on the day after Christmas.

Is the struggle worth it? Absolutely. Learning to express gratitude reminds children to consider other people's feelings rather than just their own. The purpose of thanking someone, after all, is to let that individual know how much his or her generosity and kindness are appreciated.

Being thanked in person or in a written note makes everyone feel good. In the process of composing her note to Aunt Liz, May's daughter had to consider how much time her aunt had spent making something special for her and how much she loved her aunt instead of how much she disliked the present. Thanking others is a habit we should encourage in kids.

When to write a thank-you note

Years ago, written thank-you notes were *de rigueur* in many situations. In our less formal society, a number of parents have their kids thank others by phone, which is certainly better than not thanking at all. But most manners experts today still agree that a note, even a short one, is preferable.

The general rule of thumb for gifts is this: if you open a gift when the giver is there and thank him or her in person, sending a note isn't necessary, but if you receive a present by mail or open presents later, it is. If your thirteen-year-old receives thirty presents at his bar mitzvah party and doesn't open them until everyone is gone, then he should write thirty notes to show that the gifts were received and opened.

When someone provides a very special treat for our kids, they should also write a note to express thanks. My children were taught to water-ski this past summer during a visit to my best friend and her family at their lake cottage. My friend and her

▶ PARENT TIPS

▶ "I let my daughter buy fancy, somewhat extravagant stationery—both notes and envelopes. I also supplied her with a book of stamps and her own address book," explains Sally, mother of an 11-year-old. "Now she has no excuse for not writing thank-you notes!"

▶ "When our kids get presents by mail, we make the kids write a quick thank-you note after they open each present. That way we can remember who sent what!" says Sue, mother of 6-year-old twins.

husband spent an entire day getting Annie and Alex to stand up on skis, and the day after they got home my kids wrote glowing thank-you notes without any prodding. I was delighted at their enthusiasm, even though I suspect it was partly based on the hope for another invitation next summer!

What to say in a thank-you note

A note can be simple and short. This one, written by May's nine-year-old son, contains all the essentials—date and salutation, two or three sentences that mention the present and how much you enjoy it, and a warm closing:

> December 26, 1997
>
> Dear Grandma and Grandpa,
>
> Thank you for sending me the cool Nintendo game for Christmas. I played it with Dad yesterday and I won! Hope to see you guys soon.
>
> Love, Tony

If the gift was money, your child should mention how he or she plans to spend it, as in "Now I'll be able to buy the Malibu Beach Barbie."

Notes should be written within two weeks after the event or gift—although the adage "Better late than never" is true here. Let your child, regardless of age, write the note, even if you have to write the address. Don't worry about mistakes. The sentiment is what's important. With older kids, don't make the process into an English assignment. That makes writing drudgery instead of a possibly pleasurable experience.

How to get kids to write notes

Like May, many parents find a combination of rewards, organization, and coercion usually works best. She sets aside a time, puts a box of fancy paper, pens, stamps, and envelopes on the dining room table, pulls out the address book, and insists her children finish an agreed-upon number of their notes. The reward is lemonade and cookies afterward.

According to manners experts, shortcuts like preprinted thank-you cards, where a writer only has to fill in his name and the gift item, are considered cheating. But computer-generated thank-you notes where the writer actually prints an individual note are okay as long as they are signed by hand. ❑

About Being A Good Host

When I was growing up, I used to hate the regular get-togethers of my father's side of the family because all five of my cousins were boys, and they acted totally uninterested in me. After we arrived at their house, my sister and I would dutifully follow them down to the basement "rec" room. They stayed on their side of the room, talked to each other, and played Ping-Pong, leaving us to sit by ourselves. Until my aunt came down to offer us some soda, I felt we were invisible!

My cousins have since rationalized their behavior by saying that as young boys they naturally felt shy around girls—even girl cousins—but actually that's no excuse for being a *bad* host. For kids, being a *good* host means understanding that no matter who enters your home—your best buddy from school or the dreaded children of your parents' guests—you need to use certain "host" skills to make visitors feel comfortable. Those skills are a way of saying, "I'm glad you're here."

Greet guests at the door

The first essential is welcoming a guest to your home. Some kids, like my son, are champing at the bit to see a friend and need no prompting to rush to the door when he or she arrives for a playdate. Others, who may be shy or preoccupied with a book when a friend turns up, hang back. But even a five-year-old should answer the door, say hello, act glad to see the friend, and introduce him or her to Mom and/or Dad. Experts agree that the introduction rule stands even when your thirteen-year-old daughter invites a school friend over to do homework while you and your husband are in the backyard planting shrubs. Yes, she must drag friends you've never met outside to introduce them to you! That's not necessary if you already know the friend, but it would be nice if the friend at least said hello to you.

Of course, from time to time company means relatives or children of family friends. The greeting rule holds even if your children complain, as twelve-year-old David did: "But why do I have to come down when Aunt Alice and Laura get here? Laura is only three. I don't even like her."

Offer something to eat and drink

All sorts of gestures make friends feel welcome, like showing them where to hang their jackets and backpacks, where the bathroom is, and, if they are staying overnight, where they will sleep. But perhaps the most important gesture of hospitality is offering a snack. This is another host essential, especially for kids, whose friends seem to be hungry most of the time. Nora, mother of two, solved the problem of children rummaging through the refrigerator and cupboards by simply telling her boys what they can offer.

It usually includes several choices—pretzels, crackers, cheese, apples, lemonade, and occasionally cookies and soda.

Most kids understand it's not polite to chew gum or eat a special treat they've been saving in front of a visitor without offering some, but occasionally younger kids need a reminder.

Stay with your guest!

The rule is that the host has to play with the guest during the time he's there, something younger children, like my son, forget from time to time. For example, Alex has been known to play video games enthusiastically with a friend for the first hour, then apparently grow tired of his company and, leaving him in the playroom, go outside for a bike ride! Scheduling shorter playdates for younger kids helps.

Sometimes we also have to remind our children that they can't abandon a friend they've invited. That means if they're riding bikes, your child shouldn't run off to play baseball with a neighbor they encounter—unless the guest wants to, too.

Hosts over ten years of age often can't resist chatting on the phone if another friend calls. You may have to point out they should say, "I can't talk right now I'll call you later."

Kids this age may also feel shy and act unfriendly when guests are children they don't know. Jacob's mom, like many parents, finds prompting helps. Before guests arrive, she suggests, "Pick out a few games to play with your little cousin Tyler" or "Think of something you can do with the Wilson's children."

Others just monitor the situation and, if kids can't seem to connect on any activity, step in with a board game or puzzle to get everyone playing together.

Share and cooperate

For some kids, the social skills of sharing possessions and compromising when deciding what to do are harder than they are for others. The basic rule: the guest gets to choose what to do first. Many parents closely supervise younger kids during playdates and occasionally eavesdrop on older ones. If they see their kids *aren't* sharing or cooperating, they use the opportunity to teach social politeness. When her son gets into conflicts with his friends over choosing activities, Jake's mom suggests trying those old standbys: drawing straws, flipping a coin, or just taking turns.

Most kids are better about sharing if you let them put away items they *don't* want to share before the friend arrives.

Say good-bye

Yelling "Bye!" from upstairs or the playroom doesn't count. Kids should walk their guests to the door to say good-bye and to thank them for coming. ❏

ADVICE FROM KIDS

○ "I put away my special toys—stuff like my model airplanes and my alien collection—whenever my younger cousins come over. Then I don't mind if they hang out in my room," reports Moses, 8.

○ "Always have a video ready in case the playdate gets boring," advises Amanda, 10.

○ "Get permission from your parents ahead of time so you and your friend don't have to play with your younger brother," says Lauren, 11.

○ "Don't bring your friend into your parents room or other off-limits areas or your parents will really be mad," says Nell, 13.

About Visiting & Party Manners

The flip side to teaching kids how to be good hosts is teaching them how to be good guests. Learning the first role makes learning the second much easier (and vice versa) because that gives children a way to imagine how their host might feel and develop empathy. Samantha readily recalls how she feels when her friend Eliza leaves without helping to clean up after making cookies, and Justin remembers how annoyed he was when his classmate Henry spent the afternoon playing with Justin's new computer and ignored *him*.

Saying hi to your friend when you arrive, sharing, taking turns in choosing what to do, and playing with (and not ignoring) your friend are good manners for guests as well as for hosts.

In a way, a playdate, sleepover, or party at a friend's house is a way for your child to practice the basic good manners that you've been teaching him. But the biggest manners challenge our kids face as guests is fitting in with another household's rules, routines, and plans.

Obey house rules

Every family has its own ways of doing things. In Christian's, no one is allowed to eat in the family room, even when watching a video. That means his friends can't either, even if they can at home. Sometimes our kids discover a rule only when a friend's parent tells them, as in "Mr. Roma's study is off-limits." They're usually embarrassed, but all they have to do is say, "Sorry," and remember it next time.

When your kids want something, they should ask first. Most parents, for example, don't want visitors to rummage in the refrigerator looking for a snack—they appreciate being asked. The same is true if kids need to make a phone call or want to turn on the TV or computer.

When the visit is a sleepover

Most kids, no matter what age, love to sleep over at a friend's house and want to be invited back, as Katie always is. She's a favored overnight guest because she's friendly, neat, and sensitive when others, including parents, are sleeping. After greeting everyone, she asks where to put her bag. She cleans up after herself in the bathroom, makes her bed (or rolls up her sleeping bag), and packs her things in the morning. She doesn't wake everyone up by shouting or turning up the volume of the TV. And other parents are happy to see her at breakfast, because her hair is combed, face washed, and teeth brushed.

Party manners

The first social experiences many children have are attending birthday parties. By middle school they're usually being invited to other types of parties, too, which may include their first boy-girl parties. The guidelines for guests also apply to parties, but the first party rule to teach kids is to RSVP to an invitation as soon as possible. Why? Because that makes the host's job of planning easier. Parents should reply for kids under eight years old, and until they're ten, it's best to check with the other parent yourself to make sure your child has. But if your kids are over ten, ask them, as Pat's mom does, "Did you let Margie know you're coming to her party?" (Reassure yourself that an adult will be supervising a middle-school party, though.)

When you arrive. Many of us sometimes drop our children off for a party or play-date and pick them up afterward. Since we won't be there, we may feel trepidation at the last minute. Will they have a good time? Will they just stand on the sidelines or refuse to eat the food or watch the magician? Will they be polite? This anxiety is behind our tense whispers at the front door: "Don't forget to say thank you!" "Don't ask for Pepsi instead of Coke!" and to middle schoolers, "If you feel uncomfortable for any reason, call us." The best time to instill basics, however, is long before you arrive:

- Say "Hello" to the parent or adult host.
- Say "Hi" or "Happy birthday" to the child giving the party.
- If it's a birthday party, give your present to the birthday child.

It's easy to join a party when you know everyone there, but not when you walk into a room knowing only the host. My son talks to the child host first, then breaks the ice with whoever is sitting next to him by saying, "I walk to school with Danny. How do you know him?" Having a few conversational gambits ready is essential for shy middle schoolers.

Play along and don't complain. Even if your child hates potato-sack races, he or she should join in the party activities instead of sulking on the sidelines. For middle schoolers that may mean pretending to have fun even if they aren't. No matter where the party is held, wandering off to explore is not allowed.

If your child is a fussy eater, like Lowell, who is never satisfied with what's offered, let him know that asking for substitutes at a party is impolite, unless the grown-up offers a choice, as in "Would you prefer plain pizza or one with anchovies?"

When you leave

Like many parents, I often have to remind my son to be ready to leave when I arrive to pick him up. Parents need to be prompt, too, since it not only embarrasses your child to be hanging around but also is rude to the host. Then, whether they were invited for an afternoon playdate, dinner, an overnight, or a party, kids should say good-bye and thanks to both the grown-up in charge and their friend. ❑

About Audience Manners

We've all had the experience of being in a movie theater when children—other people's, of course—have ruined the movie for us by running up and down the aisle, talking loudly, or standing and blocking the screen. "Aren't they taught any manners?" we grumble to ourselves. Those making the racket are not always packs of unsupervised kids, either; sometimes their parents are sitting right next to them, seemingly oblivious to their antics. While it's not natural for kids to sit still, unless they are taught correct audience behavior, they will experience unpleasant consequences with ushers and angry patrons.

Besides viewing feature films, your children are likely to attend many live performances as they grow up—school assemblies, recitals, the production of a musical, concerts, the sixth-grade variety show, church weddings, or a bar mitzvah with speeches. Fortunately, each experience makes the next one a bit easier.

Sit still

The first rule for being a good audience is sitting still and upright. That means feet on the floor, not underneath you or kicking the back of the seat in front of you. It also means not turning around periodically to gape at the people behind you or leaning forward so far that you're breathing down the neck of the lady in front of you. Under the seat is usually a good spot for backpacks. Put jackets on laps or let kids use them as cushions so they can see better.

Keep quiet

Being quiet is easy for kids if they're watching *Grease* with Rosie O'Donnell on Broadway; it's not so easy if they're surrounded by friends at a sister's ballet recital. That's when kids learn to practice the character-building skill of self-control. Keeping quiet means not talking during a performance (although the occasional whisper from a younger child is okay), and not giggling or pointing at someone you know on stage.

Picking appropriate performances for a child's age, level of maturity, and interests so he or she isn't bored helps. For example, even if you're dying to see the director's cut of *Lawrence of Arabia* at an art cinema, know that it's asking too much

▶ PARENT TIPS

▶ "I know you're not supposed to eat in a theater but I dole out lemon drops to keep my boys quiet," admits Gail, mother of 4.

▶ "Dress your kids comfortably!" advises Darien, mother of a preteen. "I once insisted my daughter wear a pair of dressy patent leather shoes that were so tight she took them off during the performance. They slid down to two rows in front of us, which was very embarrassing!"

of a seven-year-old to sit quietly through it for three hours. Younger kids do best at short performances geared for kids that contain plenty of action. On the other hand, a preteen passionate about music may enjoy a concert as much as an adult.

Another thing that encourages quiet is separating siblings (or friends) whenever possible. At our church's annual Lenten High Mass—which can last over an hour—our family sits in this formation: my daughter, me, my son, my husband.

Naturally, if a child has an emergency or has to go to the bathroom, he can whisper his request. But if possible, he should wait for a natural break, slip out quietly, and sit down quickly when he returns.

Prepare kids in advance

Children behave better when they know what to expect, and that includes everything from knowing what the theater will look like to the performance itself. If they're familiar with the tunes from *The Music Man,* they'll probably listen more closely and eagerly to a high-school performance of that musical (see pages 68-69).

Come early—but not too early

Kids' anxiety levels rise when they have to rush into a strange theater, with lights already dimming, but if you arrive too early, your children may become restless by the end of the first act. Try to plan on enough time to visit the restrooms and the water fountain and to look around the lobby before finding your seats. Some kids bring a book to look at or a notepad and pencil for doodling until the lights dim.

Leave if it's not working

Despite our best efforts children sometimes are completely bored and start wiggling and talking. The polite thing to do is leave as soon as you can, as Paul's parents did when it was clear Paul was uninterested in the ballet *Giselle* and was disturbing others. They knew that forcing him to sit through it would make it a negative experience for him, too, and keep him from wanting to try again in the future. ❏

About School Manners

Peter, a third grader, is happy at school—most of the time—and his teacher is happy with him. Though no one would call Peter a goody-goody, he greets her with "Hello, Mrs. Speranzo" and a grin, his daily vocabulary in class includes "please" and "thank you," and if a teacher asks him to take a message to the school office, he cheerfully complies. The truth is, if our children are polite and respectful to their teachers, other school personnel, and other kids, as Peter generally is, they're much more likely to be successful both in schoolwork and with their classmates.

That's why it's important to coach your child in the manners and social skills he or she needs in school. How to do this? First, remember that when kids practice basic good manners at home, they take these habits with them to school. And second, we can make sure our children know what special kinds of polite behavior teachers expect and like, and why.

Raise your hand

The single most common complaint teachers have about kids' manners in the classroom is that so many children yell out, "I know the answer!" or ask, "What was that?" before they are called on. With twenty or thirty children in a class, this kind of behavior is bound to disrupt class discussion. Like all interrupting, it's impulsive and often a sign of immaturity.

Raising your hand and waiting to be called on—which is what teachers want children to do—takes self-control as well as a recognition that what other kids have to say is important, too.

While teachers are more tolerant of kids' yelling out in the earlier grades, it makes a negative impression on them. Parents can help kids practice self-control at home and teach them *polite* ways to get an adult's attention (see pages 40-45 and 73-75).

Follow instructions and pay attention

Much of school involves doing what some-one in authority—a teacher or principal or playground supervisor—asks you to do. Some kids, like Peter, readily go along without arguing, whether they feel like it or not, while others, like T. J., frequently challenge requests with a wisecrack or smart remark. This may impress peers, at least initially, but our kids need to know that sassing and talking back will get them in trouble with teachers and that their parents will take steps to stop it.

Another way children—and adults—show respect for others is by paying attention to what they say. When Patricia whispers or passes notes to her best friend while Mr. Wool is explaining something during the sixth-grade math class, she is not only showing bad manners in how she treats the teacher, but she's distracting other children from learning—and herself as well.

How to disagree with a teacher

Teachers usually say that they don't mind kids' disagreeing or correcting them; it's the way they do it that can be bad manners. When the teacher mispronounced Diane Flyum's last name while taking attendance on the first day of school, Diane said quietly, with a smile, "It's pronounced 'Flem.'" That smile is crucial because it's a signal to the teacher that no disrespect is meant. Middle schoolers especially need to know that disagreeing in a calm way—"Didn't you say the book report wasn't due until next Friday, Ms. Rogers?"—gets a better response than shouting angrily, "You said next Friday! You can't change it now!"

Ask nicely for help or permission

A school librarian I know admits that she automatically gives twice the help to a smiling, polite, soft-spoken child than she does to a sullen, demanding one. So do most teachers. Jerry discovered that if he asks nicely by looking his science teacher in the eye, smiling, and asking in a pleasant voice, "Would it be okay if I did my report on whales instead of sharks?" she's much more likely to say, "Of course." Kids like Jerry are the ones the librarian saves a special book for and the teacher chooses for a special job or privilege.

How to behave in the cafeteria

Even the most polite children often forget their manners at lunch. So it's a good idea to remind kids of several important rules. One is no cutting in the cafeteria line. It's easy for a fifth grader to muscle ahead of a second grader, but it's not fair. Loudly complaining and making fun of the food when food workers can hear is deliberately hurting feelings. Comments about "mystery meat" or "orange glue" on the grilled cheese sandwiches can wait till kids are sitting down with friends. While few schools expect the napkin-on-the-lap level of table manners, throwing food and food fights are universally condemned. Being considerate means cleaning up, too, by throwing away garbage and returning food trays.

Don't tease other kids

To be happy and productive in school, our children need to be able to get along with others, many of whom are not their best friends. We can all identify the manners and social skills kids need. Be friendly. Share. Disagree without getting angry. Don't hit or brag. And especially important, be kind—don't tease others about their glasses, weight, or big nose, doing poorly on a quiz, or being a klutz on the basketball court (see pages 84-86). Popular Erin goes along with her mom's motto: "If you can't say anything nice about someone, don't say anything at all." ❑

ADVICE FROM KIDS

○ "Don't yell across tables," says Kate, 6.

○ "Say hello to the cafeteria lady and she'll look for the best slice of pizza to give you!" advises Vincent, 7.

○ "Never ask someone what they got on a quiz. It's embarrassing to admit to a low grade," suggests Kevin, age 11.

○ "Say hello to teachers you had last year—you never know when you might need a recommendation!" says Andrea, 13.

About Sportsmanship

Both my son and daughter play on community-sponsored soccer teams, and my husband and I regularly attend their games. We've noticed that although most of the kids act like good sports most of the time, at each game there are always several instances of temper tantrums and nasty barbs directed at referees, the opposing team, and even teammates. Surprisingly, some parents frequently show worse sportsmanship than their own children—they talk back to the ref, question the coaches' decisions, and even badger children on the opposing team.

In elementary and middle school, kids begin to participate in all kinds of sports and games, from Monopoly to soccer, and as a result, competition becomes a big part of their lives. How they handle winning and losing, following the rules, playing fair, and being a member of a team determine whether they'll be respected and valued players or not. If they learn to be good sports, they will find that everyone wants them on a team. If they don't, they're liable to be teased or rejected by their peers, even if they're good at making a goal or a touchdown.

Since one way our kids learn how to behave on the field is by watching us, we can start teaching them sports manners by being on our best sports behavior, too.

Play by the rules

The boys in the Center School fifth grade don't want Aaron in their recess games because, they say, "Aaron cheats!" Playing fair and following the rules are very important to children in the five-to-thirteen age group, and they are quick to reject those who don't. We can help kids by praising them for playing by the rules and reminding them—frequently—that trying your best is what's most important.

Share equipment

Being willing to share equipment is essential if kids want to get invited to play games and become a team member. If they use a friend's bat or tennis racket, it should be returned with a smile and a thank you.

► PARENT TIPS

► "After my daughter's soccer games, I ask her to describe plays she made with other teammates, rather than concentrating on whether her team won or lost," reports Belinda, mother of a 6-year-old.

► "We checked around until we found teams with coaches who stress cooperation instead of competition. We didn't want so much pressure on our kids," say Marty and Jane, parents of a 5- and a 7-year-old.

► "When I'm playing ball with my son and he gets so frustrated that he slams down the bat or glove, I make him sit on the sidelines for a moment—I call it the 'seat of forgiveness'—to cool down, forget about mistakes, and be ready to start again," says Ray, father of 3.

No arguing with the ref

It's frustrating for any player when the referee makes a wrong or unfair call. But the rule in all sports—from kindergarten soccer to professional baseball—is the ref's decision stands, *no matter what*. Unfortunately kids often observe professional players and coaches—and even their own parents—flouting this rule.

It's up to us to help kids understand that accepting a referee's call is part of playing by the rules.

Don't show off or brag

It's not easy for kids to restrain their natural self-centeredness. Witness my neighbor's daughter, who screamed, "I made a goal! That's why our team won!" as she came off the field at the end of a game.

I saw several of her teammates exchange annoyed glances, and finally, one said, "Yeah, but I assisted—you couldn't have done it without me."

Another added, "Yeah, and Marlene kept the ball close so you could assist."

The coach explained that showing off and bragging were signs of a weak player. He added, "Playing on a team means taking both credit and blame together."

We can encourage our kids to compliment teammates who helped them make a goal or slam dunk by saying, "Thanks for the assist" or "Great set-up." Remind them, too, that no one likes someone who brags.

Watch out for others

Showing consideration for others is also being careful around them. That means when Jordan is skiing he should look ahead to make sure he won't mow down someone in front of him. The same holds for boogie boarding, Rollerblading, and other sports. Of course, accidents do happen. But if Jordan knocks down another skier or causes him to fall, sports etiquette dictates that he should go to him, apologize, and find help, if necessary. The same applies to other sports.

Winning and losing

Most kids want to win and hate to lose. But if your child sulks and complains, angrily throws down his equipment, or blames a teammate when his team loses, he will find himself called a poor loser. Kids don't like those who gloat and carry on too much when they win, the way Freddy used to, either. Finally his dad told him in private, "You're making the other kids feel bad by the way you're acting."

Win or lose, sportsmanship means congratulating your opponent for playing well, whether the game is chess or softball. In team sports most coaches line up the two teams to pass by "slapping five" and saying—cheerfully!—"Good game." Your child may not feel like being cheerful, but you can encourage him to put his personal feelings aside to be a good sport. ❑

About Clothing & Grooming Manners

A big part of good manners is showing respect toward others, and a big part of showing respect is having a neat and clean appearance. For kids that doesn't mean expensive clothes and salon coiffures, but it does mean clean fingernails, a washed face, fresh breath, a freshly bathed body, and clean hair and clothes.

Showing respect also means dressing appropriately, which translates into matching the clothes to the occasion. Isaac's faded sweatpants and baggy shirt are acceptable attire in his second-grade classroom but wouldn't be at his aunt Pam's wedding.

These distinctions aren't always clear to younger kids, which is why we need to teach grooming and impose clothing standards for certain situations. With kids in middle school, the war is often between their standards and ours.

What about grooming?

Being clean is the bottom line, no matter what a child's age and where he or she is going. Most kids—especially younger boys—appear incredulous when they are told, "That shirt is filthy; put on a clean one." "But Mom—" they wail indignantly, looking down at the ground-in dirt, bicycle grease, and spilled grape juice. "It *is* clean!" You will never convince such a child that, in fact, the shirt will soon be walking on its own. If he is building a fort in your

backyard with his buddies, however, so what? But if he is heading for school or a party, making him change the shirt and wash up are an essential part of teaching him grooming.

The most obvious place to enforce grooming standards is at the dinner table. Check out face, hands, fingernails, and hair, and send children back to the bathroom to redo if they missed a spot or have hair hanging in their faces. After being sent back repeatedly to rewash and recomb, they'll eventually get the hang of it, and hopefully remember when they eat at someone else's house.

For middle-school kids entering puberty, body odor is a reality, even if they don't realize it. A daily shower should be a requirement. Letting children pick out their own soap and shampoo sometimes encourages more frequent showers and hair-washing. I try to make grooming easier by giving each child a shelf in the linen closet on which to keep his or her own supplies, such as nailbrush, shampoo, comb, towels, and soap.

Setting an example also helps. When leaving the house with your children, pause at the mirror to comb your own hair, tuck in shirttails, and adjust collars.

What's appropriate dress?

The hard part for parents is knowing when to let kids experiment with clothes—and thereby develop taste and style—and when to step in and stop them from looking inappropriate. A good rule is to give more leeway when your child will be among his peers—when he's going to a friend's party—and to set higher standards when he'll be around adults. For most of those occasions that means clean clothes that aren't torn and no T-shirts with cartoon characters. Negotiation is often necessary. If your family is eating out, your twelve-year-old son might be willing to wear khakis instead of worn jeans if you let him wear his clean "Bad Dog" T-shirt. But kids shouldn't wear hats at the table! In fact, many adults still expect them to remove hats when they enter any building.

For more formal occasions such as a holiday gathering, clothes should be dressier. My kids sit docilely as I whip out the velvet dress and the button-down shirt because they know resistance is useless. One mother of two preteen girls allows choices provided they fulfill her minimum requirements. But many parents have stringent rules about what clothes show proper respect in a church or synagogue. Usually that means no T-shirts, baseball caps, shorts, low-cut tops, or anything flashy.

Your community affects the choice, too. In a conservative one, even younger boys may be expected to wear button-down shirts to a fancy party, while in a casual one, a nice polo shirt is dressy enough.

▶ PARENT TIPS

▶ "My son wears his baseball hat everywhere. Finally we negotiated. He takes it off for special dinners, when we have guests, and in church. Otherwise he can wear it," says Eve, mother of a 10-year-old.

▶ "My 11-year-old is obsessed with nail polish. We made a rule that she couldn't wear it to school, but on the weekends she could go crazy with her favorite purple and green polish," explains Fran, mother of 2 girls.

Fitting in at school

To most kids, especially preteens, wearing appropriate clothes means wearing exactly what their classmates wear. What's fashionable-yet-okay for school varies considerably from community to community. I try to remember, when checking out my kids in the morning, that the two most important words in clothing and grooming manners are "clean" and "neat." If they pass that test, I let them out the door.

But we should also make our kids aware that some clothes and excessive makeup generally communicate negative messages to adults, even if they're the norm among their friends. The way Jack wears his baseball hat in class shows his defiant attitude toward authority. And adults—and most kids—assume an eleven-year-old girl who wears a sexy belly shirt, mascara, and fake nails is ready to party, not study. ❏

Plan Ahead For Special Occasions

The best way to ensure that kids use a new social skill is to give them a chance to practice it with you before they have to perform in public. As all parents know, we can lecture our children on what to do, but that doesn't mean they'll remember or be able to follow through and do the right thing when it counts. Just like adults, they fall back on old habits when they're in unfamiliar situations and feel uncomfortable.

By acting out events ahead of time, kids can learn to talk politely to Uncle Al, who wears a hearing aid and shouts his questions, or even feel at ease attending a wedding dinner for the first time. Brief dress rehearsals are just as useful for common scenarios as for special occasions. Guy, for example, helped his shy eight-year-old daughter figure out how to ask the supermarket owner if her Girl Scout troop could set up a table in the market to sell raffle tickets.

One key is discussing upcoming activities with your kids. If your thirteen-year-old son is competing in a tournament, you can suggest, "Think about what you'll say to your friends if you win." For special situations, anticipate what your children may need to know.

Special visits

We have friends whose pristine home reflects their childless lifestyle: white carpet and couches, porcelain figurines, glass cocktail table. The first time they invited all of us

for dinner—when my son was five and my daughter seven—the visit was a disaster. I hadn't prepared my children or brought any quiet games, and as a result my son almost broke a figurine and my daughter entertained herself by leaving fingerprints all over the glass table.

Now I remind my kids to choose something to bring to entertain themselves, such as a deck of cards, markers and paper, or a book, and we also talk about things our hosts may do. For example, when visiting an elderly relative, you might want to say in the car en route, "Aunt Becky will want to hug you and kiss you a lot when we arrive and will ask about school. Can you think of some interesting things to tell her?" If you remind them she now uses a walker, they won't gape.

Practice is equally useful if relatives or old friends your children don't know are coming to visit you.

A special dinner or party

Whether you're going to a party at a fancy restaurant or attending a wedding brunch, it's important to describe it as much as possible and practice briefly the skills kids, especially younger ones, will need. Matilda set aside a family dinner for her kids to rehearse how to behave at her cousin's wedding dinner. Her husband, Bob, played the maître d' and walked them to the table. The place settings included more silver than usual, and Matilda put out the food on a sideboard so they could practice for the buffet. The kids had plenty of questions: What's a toast? If there's dancing, do we get to dance? The more they know, the better children behave.

Performances and ceremonies

Most kids don't attend ceremonies and professional performances that often. But when they do, preparation helps (see pages 60-61). We'd told our kids that the theater at Lincoln Center in New York City, where we were seeing *The Nutcracker* ballet, was big. My son, who loves maps, relaxed after checking out our seat placement on the diagram. Hearing a plot summary of the ballet and the musical highlights a few days before kept them from asking us questions during the performance.

Preteens feel especially nervous about attending ceremonies of religions that aren't their own for the first time. When my neighbor's son was invited to a friend's bar mitzvah, his whole family learned about the ceremony from a video in our local library. And when my daughter had a first communion party, one smart mom phoned me the week before to ask about the ceremony and the party afterward.

Another good preparation tactic is for kids to watch a movie that features a child with social poise, like *The Karate Kid*, and pretend they are that character. ❑

AGE FACTOR

Manners are learned throughout childhood, and at each age children need to know new social skills.

❖ At 5 and 6, kids can practice saying hello to Daddy's or Mommy's co-workers.

❖ Eight- and 9-year-olds should practice manners for a sleepover.

❖ Kids 8 and older can be taught what to expect at a hospital visit or a funeral service.

When Your Child Is Rude

There are generally two ways we discover our children are being rude, and both require our attention. One is when we see or hear the rude behavior ourselves, as Margaret did when she drove her eleven-year-old daughter, Kate, and two friends home from the variety show rehearsal. Just about every comment Kate made bad-mouthed a classmate in the show. Margaret counted the catty remarks. The score: Kate, twenty-five, her friends, six.

The other is when we hear about our children's rudeness from someone else. For example, your mother reports that she "was appalled" by her granddaughter's table manners after your six-year-old visited her for a weekend. Or the fifth-grade teacher informs you at a conference that your son regularly brags about the A grades he receives on tests. Or even more embarrassing, a good friend calls to confide that she was upset at your son's use of curse words while at her house.

Don't ignore rude behavior

To stop kids' rude behavior, experts say, we have to address it when we see or hear about it, whether kids are rude to us, to their friends, or at school. Easier said than done, since it takes time and effort to address rude remarks or actions. But we do our kids no favor by continually ignoring their rudeness, because other people in their world certainly won't!

Why kids are rude

The first step is letting kids know what they've done and why it's rude, and determining why they did it. Often the reason is a lack of certain social skills. Five-year-old David didn't know the proper way to act when a friend of his dad's asked him a question to which he didn't know the answer. So he just stood there, silent and uncommunicative. "Adults think it's rude if kids don't answer a direct question," his mom explained sympathetically. "Next time, just answer politely, 'I don't know.'"

Sometimes, of course, our children are highly aware of what they've done—they *choose* to act rudely because it gets them attention, makes them feel big and important for a moment, or gets a laugh. James likes impressing his friends with how tough he is by dropping the F word into his conversation at every opportunity. When rudeness is deliberate, we need to set consequences as well as tell kids that, for example, it's not respectful to use swear words in front of your friend's mom.

Defining rudeness

Identifying rudeness can occasionally be tricky. As we all know, different people have higher or lower tolerances of certain behaviors—you may not care if your six-year-old leaves the table without asking to be excused, while her grandma does care. Also, kids' interpretations of what's rude often differ from ours. "Everyone calls the substitute by his first name," your child may tell you reassuringly.

Kids like Kate often defend their nasty comments with the line, "Oh, Mom, they know I was just kidding." It's true, teasing can be playful, but if it hurts someone's feelings, it's definitely rude. Here are some typical ways kids are rude:

- calling someone a bad name
- not saying hello on the phone or in person
- not saying thank you or please
- ignoring a direct question
- interrupting a grown-up conversation
- starting to eat before mom and dad sit
- not helping to clear the table after dinner at a friend's house
- hogging the remote control when watching TV
- pointing at a person in a wheelchair
- borrowing a friend's magazine or sweater and not returning it promptly
- popping bubble gum in someone's face
- booing the other team when they score
- cutting in a popcorn line at the movies
- leaving clothes in a heap on the floor of the fitting room
- not getting out of the way so an adult or child can pass easily on the street
- cutting off a passerby on a bicycle or Rollerblades
- talking back to the bus driver
- yelling or gesturing to passing cars

Say what to do—and what not to do

Encouraging with do's rather than scolding with don'ts is more effective in correcting kids' manners, especially when they don't know they are being rude. If you hear your child grunt into the phone, reminding him with "Say hello politely when you pick up the phone" generally works much better than complaining, "Why can't you ever answer the telephone properly?"

But we also have to let kids know certain kinds of behavior are unacceptable. For example, bad-mouthing and criticizing others are common among school-age kids. Kate's mom said, "You know, Kate, the way you were talking about your friends was rude and unkind. Insults and nasty remarks get back to people. If you hurt your friends' feelings, they'll stop wanting to be friends with you." This may make Kate think twice the next time she's tempted to bad-mouth someone.

If your child is rude, reprimand with a whisper ("Don't point at that man with the scar on his face") or in private. One mom I know has a code phrase, "hot fudge," that she uses as a warning if her kids go into a rude mode when in public or with friends. That way she gets her no-rudeness message across without embarrassing them.

Accepting invitations

It's often difficult to make sure our children are being polite to friends, especially as

ADVICE FROM KIDS

Here are some ways kids combat rudeness:

- "I let the new kid sit next to me on the bus even though no one else would," reports Alan, 6.

- "When someone cuts in line, I put my foot out and say 'Sorry, we were all here first' and look at the rest of the line like they're all on my side," explains Paul, 9.

- "I waited till after class to tell my teacher that her slip was showing so she wouldn't get embarrassed," says Hannah, 11.

they get older. But we can certainly *prevent* rudeness by setting a rule and sticking to it when it comes to the better-invitation problem. For example, ten-year-old Tara makes a plan to spend Saturday at her friend Naomi's house. Then Patty calls to invite Tara to go to the mall on Saturday, which Tara would much rather do. She tells her mom, "I'll call Naomi and say I can't come over after all. Then I can go with Patty."

Tara's mom won't let her daughter accept the second invitation and says firmly, as most parents would, "That's rude. The rule in our family is that you keep the commitment you made or invitation you accepted first."

Set rules and consequences

Just about all kids find it easier to be polite when we establish clear, specific rules and follow through with consequences. Of course, we have to keep a sense of proportion about this—and not make a seven-year-old eat in the kitchen alone just because he forgets to put his napkin on his lap. But if a few warnings don't do the trick, resist nagging and impose penalties or take away privileges—and make sure kids know in advance what these will be. This tactic is especially necessary when our kids are deliberately rude. If a child keeps teasing a friend, for example, forbid play-dates for a few days. If he hurts someone's

feelings, ask him to find a way to make it up. Consequences can be positive, too—if your son often forgets to say thank you, be sure to offer praise when he remembers.

When your children are rude to you

Kids are more likely to be rude to us when their friends are around. Why? They're showing off and testing our limits. But experts—and most parents—agree that we shouldn't allow our kids to be disrespectful to us. If we do, we're training them to be that way to other adults, such as babysitters and teachers. Tanya's mom told her daughter, "You can hate me, but you can't speak to me in that fresh way. If you do it in front of your friends, be prepared to be embarrassed." If your child is in the habit of being rude to you, set consequences!

Work with the teacher

Let your kids know your rules about rudeness extend to their behavior at school, too. When Brian's mom learned he and apparently the entire class had been rude to the substitute teacher and Brian thought it was hilarious, she met with his regular third-grade teacher to discuss Brian's behavior. Was Brian often rude in class? The answer was yes. The two of them developed a plan with Brian to curb his inappropriate jokes. The bottom line: if Brian was rude, he stayed in for recess and lost an hour of TV watching at home. ❏

When I asked a group of mothers at a soccer game what was the most irritating bad-manners habit their kids had, all twelve agreed: "When my son/daughter interrupts, it drives me crazy!"

Here's a typical example. Your child is completely occupied—watching television or playing a game. You pick up the phone in the next room, and just as you start a conversation with your best friend or the credit card company, your child comes in and demands your attention for a very important "emergency"—there's no more cranberry juice or he needs to talk about his Halloween costume even though it's only May. Your reaction, like that of most parents, is an angry, "Can't you see I'm on the phone? Why can't you ever wait?"

Interrupting us when we're on the telephone is just one of the many ways children engage in this annoying behavior. We *can* stop it, but that takes patience and perseverance.

Why kids interrupt

Young children often interrupt conversations because they aren't sophisticated enough to sense when a person is finished talking. As they mature, they learn to recognize natural breaks. In the meantime, it helps to say, "Just a minute, honey. I'm not finished yet."

Other children, including older ones, interrupt because they can't hold on to a train of thought for any length of time. That's why so many first graders complain, "When the teacher finally called on me, I forgot what I was going to say!"

Then there are the kids, like Roy, who interrupt because they want attention. Whenever his mom is doing something for his stepbrother, Roy suddenly barges in with, "I need help, Mom!" Since young children have a limited ability to see other people's needs, they're usually convinced that what they want to ask or say is more important than what anyone else does.

Most of the time, however, our kids interrupt for the same reason some adults do: because they don't have the self-control to wait. And if no one teaches them to wait, interrupting becomes a habit that's tough to break, one that will get them in trouble at school as well as with friends.

Just say no

Experts advise that the best way to stop the interrupting habit is not to let children break into your conversation. On paper, that looks easy, but in real life it's not. The hardest part is being consistent in enforcing the no-interrupting rule. If you observe any conversation between adults or children, you'll see how readily people allow interruptions.

However, if you regularly let it slide, kids eventually learn that if they just persist, sooner or later they'll be rewarded with

second warning. Three fingers mean a one-minute time-out. This may sound harsh, yet it's so effective in my house that I rarely have to resort to the time-out.

Other parents simply remind kids of what they're doing and tell them when they *can* talk, as in "Deirdre, you're pulling on my sleeve and interrupting my talk with Daddy. Come back in five minutes and then I'll listen to what you have to tell me." Be sure you follow through five minutes later—and praise children for waiting patiently!

For chronic interrupters who are very demanding, though, more serious consequences such as losing a privilege are sometimes necessary.

When two kids talk at the same time

My kids, like many siblings, are fiercely competitive and interrupt each other at every opportunity, especially at the dinner table. If I ask Annie how her sore throat is, Alex pipes up that it hurts to swallow as she replies. If I ask Alex how he did on his spelling test, Annie blurts out that she got a 90 on hers while Alex is still talking.

your attention. A good way to begin is to use a gesture or code word to warn your kids just as they're about to interrupt. I use the arm straight out, palm-vertical motion similar to the one Diana Ross uses as she sings "Stop In the Name of Love." This works especially well if I'm on the phone because I can keep talking. If my kids continue to interrupt, I hold up one finger as a warning. Two fingers is a

74

One way I've found to stop this kind of behavior is to hold up my arm in front of the offending child and say, "Let Annie finish" or "Alex first, then you." The important part is to always make good on a promise to return to the second child by saying, "Okay, your turn now." That way kids know that although they must wait, they *will* be heard.

Interrupting friends

Often kids forget that you have to take turns when talking with a friend just as you do when playing with a toy or choosing a video game.

Talkative and opinionated kids, like Sarah, sometimes bulldoze over attempts by a friend to venture an opinion and seem oblivious even to obvious signs that a friend doesn't like being constantly interrupted. Sarah's friend, Rachel, for example, eventually stops trying to talk altogether, looks glum, and ends up going home earlier than planned.

When Sarah's mom realized how frequently her daughter interrupted and how bossy it made her appear to her friends, she first shared her observations sympathetically with Sarah. To help Sarah, she suggested her daughter try looking directly at a friend's face as she talked, concentrate on listening to what her friend said, and make sure that after Sarah said one thing, she let her friend talk next.

▶ PARENT TIPS

▶ "When I'm on the telephone, the only interruptions I allow are those written on a piece of paper. My son hands me a note like 'Can I go next door to Petey's house?' I can read it and nod yes or no without breaking my conversation," reports Mike, father of 3.

▶ "After my divorce my daughter started interrupting my date whenever he spoke. I finally realized Sara felt she wasn't getting to spend enough time with me. Now I try to make sure we have enough time for conversations when she wants to talk," says Mary, a single parent of a 10-year-old.

▶ "I use the same techniques at home that I do in my 2nd-grade class. At family meetings, the kids raise their hands until I call on one of them— otherwise, there would be complete chaos!" says Ginny, mother of 4.

The polite way to interrupt

Of course there are circumstances where you want your child to interrupt you—for example, in an emergency, such as when there's smoke coming out of the oven. But we need to instruct kids to do it politely by starting with the words "excuse me," as in "Excuse me, Mom, but there's smoke coming out of the oven." The quickest way to establish this habit is to try to turn to your child immediately whenever he says, "Excuse me, mom, but . . ." and pay attention to what he says. Of course, some kids simply use "excuse me" as an automatic interrupter. So it usually helps to define what you mean by "emergency," too. ❏

When Your Child Uses Bad Words & Makes Noises

My son's former kindergarten teacher loves to tell the story of the time she took his class to visit the town's firehouse. On the way, the school bus was stalled in traffic, and my son—a normally soft-spoken little boy—suddenly shouted, "Sonofabitch, sonofabitch, sonofabitch!" and explained, "That's what Daddy says to make the traffic go away."

While this may seem amusing if a child is five years old, it's not funny if he is ten. The moral, of course, is that parents have to be very aware of the language *they* use, because whenever you do something you *don't* want your children to do, you can be sure they will copy it. Even if you don't say, "Damn it," your kids will hear cursing, belching, and much more from their friends on the school bus and at the playground—and join in. Being one of the gang in elementary and middle school means saying and doing things together that adults don't approve of. But that doesn't mean we have to permit rude language and noises in front of us!

The "bad" language problem

What's bad language in your house? To most parents it means swear words and the bathroom talk that delights five-, six-, and seven-year-olds—"poo-poo," etc. Some parents, like Will, the father of three, also include derogatory words and phrases such as "Stupid," "I hate you!" "You're dumb," "Shut up," "That sucks," and more.

When kids use any of these, their aim is often simply to get a rise out of parents and teachers—middle schoolers seem to think the F word and any other references to sex sound cool and sophisticated. Bad language is also used by people of all ages as a kind of catharsis when they're angry. It's a precursor to outbursts of temper, too. The boy who can't resist swearing on the tennis court is also likely to be the one who flings down his racket and stomps off in a huff.

"We don't use those words"

"If parents don't address inappropriate language, it escalates and may become a habit," explains Sandra Loughran, a psychologist and Montessori teacher. The way to do it, she says, is to give a calm, unemotional reprimand, such as "We don't use language like that." If that doesn't suffice,

▶ PARENT TIPS

- ▶ "Our house rule: if a word is allowed on network TV, it's allowed in our house," says Vicky, mother of 2.

- ▶ "We have a penalty system. Whoever swears gets a check after their name on a chart in the kitchen—parents get 2 checks. Anyone with 5 or more checks has to do an extra chore," say Wendy and Zach, parents of 3.

she suggests parents say, "Go to your room and think about what you're really trying to say." Will taught his kids alternative expletives to use when angry—"rubbish" and "rats"—and when they say, "It sucks," asks them to rephrase the sentence.

Most experts advise parents to forget about trying to control their child's language when they are not around them and concentrate on what kids say at the dinner table, to their face, and in public with other adults.

What are rude noises?

Like many parents, I divide burping, belching, stomach rumblings, and farting into two categories: involuntary noises and those done with intent. The second is the offense. Obviously, we shouldn't make a child feel guilty because his body simply reacted the wrong way. But we can teach our kids how to respond if it does.

When Larry accidentally burps at dinner, for example, all he needs to say is "Excuse me" as calmly as possible— not call attention to his burp by acting out over-the-top mortification! Larry's sister should not, as she and most kids usually do, burst into giggles, but instead ignore it and go on with the conversation.

If parents excuse themselves when they inadvertently burp or pass gas kids will eventually pick up on this and do likewise, though reminders help.

When it's deliberate

Deliberately making rude noises, on the other hand, shows disrespect just as using bad language does. Whether our kids do it at home or during circle time at school, their purpose is to make adults uncomfortable and to get attention. That's why it's important not to reward an "arm fart" with laughter even if your husband is privately impressed his son was able to master this incredible feat. When my son turned six, he somehow learned how to belch on demand, and overnight he became the king of first grade. He showed us at dinner, he tried it at church, and demonstrated it to my parents. Finally my husband said that was enough. Alex could belch in his bedroom, in the bathroom, and whenever he was alone in a room, but nowhere else. So far, so good. α

About Private Behavior & Privacy

Teaching kids how to tell the difference between what they can do in public and what behavior should be done alone—in the privacy of the bathroom or their own bedroom—is a delicate subject area. Some parents are so uncomfortable that they simply ignore the whole subject. Other parents bear the scars of a guilt-ridden childhood in which everything to do with one's body was considered bad or dirty, and as a result they allow their kids to walk around picking their noses and scratching themselves—to the dismay of teachers and other adults. Still others go in the opposite direction. Worried that their children will appear uncivilized, they ban everything from public nose-blowing to hair-combing.

Anyone with children can agree that the body *is* beautiful. After all, we watch our children's bodies develop from birth to puberty, and we are awed at the perfection of their form. Our job as parents is to teach children when to be private without teaching them to be ashamed of their body or their body functions.

Personal care is private

It's considered good manners for kids (and adults) to engage in personal care activities we associate with the bathroom in private: for example, brushing and flossing teeth or picking food out of

braces, bathing and showering, applying deodorant, changing clothes, and going to the bathroom. It's rude to announce to everyone in the room what you are going to do in the bathroom— "I have to take a leak"—the way one preteen boy I know does. And no one really wants to watch thirteen-year-old Rhonda checking out her pimples at the dinner table or observe Nathaniel cutting his toenails on the family room couch while watching TV. Why? As one twelve-year-old informed her brother, "Because it's gross." Nose-picking is, too, but rest assured that it's a very normal habit in both boys and girls in the five-to-thirteen age group. Like many parents, you may find yourself repeating, "Please get a tissue and do that in the bathroom" for many years.

Masturbation is private, too

Seeing children fondle themselves in public makes most adults uncomfortable, even if the kids are very young. For toddlers, preschoolers, and even five- and six-year-olds, holding their genitals is often a soothing act—much the same way thumb-sucking is comforting. Most teachers and psychologists believe that masturbation is part of children's natural discovery process in learning about their bodies, and some even regard it as a healthy response to the incredible stress children undergo in our society these days.

If you do observe a child fondling herself or himself in public, offer a reminder that this is not public behavior without embarrassing the child. Experts suggest saying, "That's something you do in private," in a neutral tone of voice. Usually that's all that's necessary. In fact, most kids over the age of six know this is something for their own room.

Respecting privacy

Good manners include respecting others' privacy as well as one's own. In other words, it's just as important to respect a closed door when your child is in the bathroom as it is to teach him or her when the door ought to be closed. All kids will be more respectful of others' privacy if they receive privacy in turn.

But we have to let our kids know what we consider private. Joanne, for example, doesn't mind if her daughter Lindsay sits at her dressing table and tries on all her makeup and perfume as long as Lindsay asks first. On the other hand, like most of us, Joanne doesn't want Lindsay or her brother to listen in on her telephone conversations via the extension, read a letter from her best friend, or rummage through the desk drawer where she keeps her bills.

There is such a thing as a child being respectful of his own body, too. If your neighbor puts his arm around your child and she doesn't like it, she's not being rude if she quietly moves away from him without making a fuss. If Andrew wants to be alone in his bedroom with the door closed, his mom or dad should not barge in without knocking, or, as some parents do, barge in *while* knocking. Children can say, "I'd rather try the jeans on in the fitting room by myself, Aunt Kathy," for example, as long as they say it respectfully and with a smile. ❏

79

When Your Child's Friend Has Bad Manners

Gabe's mom is not very enthusiastic about her eight-year-old son's new best friend, Nick. Why? For one thing, he's very demanding when he comes over to play. "Why don't you ever have anything good to eat?" he rudely asks when she offers crackers, cheese, and several kinds of juice, and then he starts pawing through the refrigerator himself. Nor does he say thank you, not even when she drives him (and his bike!) home because it's raining, as she has several times.

Like Gabe's mom, many parents who work hard to instill good manners in their children find it annoying when a playmate displays bad manners. We can do something about it, but not too much.

In your house

When your child's friend shows poor manners during a playdate at *your* house, the way Nick did, there are ways to correct the behavior tactfully. One way is to have basic "house rules" and regularly refer to them, as in "Nick, the rule in our house is that we hang up jackets" or "Honey, we don't use those words in our house." That gets your point across without hurting feelings or worse, insulting your child's guest. Even though I know my rules may not change

the child's behavior completely, it might change his behavior *while* he's in my home, and that's really enough for me.

Making mild suggestions works too. I sometimes say, "Here's your napkin—you can put in on your lap like this" to a playmate who is staying for dinner, and "I'd rather you ask me first before you take paper from my desk." And I praise and thank children when they do.

Not to make these corrections sends a mixed message to our kids. When we maintain our standards for good manners regardless of

a friend's behavior, our kids feel comfortable knowing that the rules don't change. That's why we remind them that even if the rest of the class, or the bus, or the puppet show audience is being rude, we still expect them to show respect and remember their manners.

When a child's parent is present

Correcting another child's behavior when his or her parent is sitting right next to you at the park or fast-food restaurant, however, is generally considered bad manners on your part. If a child spits out French fries, burps deliberately, or uses a curse word, and his mom or dad says nothing, you can't say anything to the child, either. But if both kids are blowing straw covers at the kids at the next table, you can certainly say to your own child, as one mom did, "Tony! If you don't stop that, we'll have to leave."

Some parents try to discuss a child's rudeness with the parent in a non-threatening way, as in "Boy, it really gets to me when my kids do that. Does it bother you? How do you handle that?" If the other parent is a good friend, of course, this is much easier to do.

Experts suggest that you discuss a rude friend situation with your child later, as Tony's mom did, and point out how a friend's bad manners affected others. But be careful to criticize the friend's manners rather than the friend. Preteens in particular will often leap to their friend's defense out of loyalty.

Other rude friend problems

Sometimes kids are the ones who are uncomfortable with a friend's rudeness. Ten-year-old Beth loved visiting her friend Renee's grandmother's house because the two girls were allowed to try on all her grandma's old clothes in the attic. "The only problem," Beth told her mom after her first visit, "is that Renee is not very nice to her grandma." She explained how Renee bossed her grandma around and demanded petulantly, "Grandma, I said I wanted an ice-pop! And get another one for Beth!" Beth didn't say anything at the time, but she felt bad about it.

What your child can do

Even though children criticize each other all the time, no child wants to be thought of as a goody-goody. Beth's mom pointed out that the next time Beth could say politely, "Renee, your grandma was nice to invite us over. If I talked to my grandma in that bossy way she'd kill me! We should get the ice-pops ourselves." Then Beth could go up to Renee's grandmother and say, "Thanks for the ice-pop" with a big smile. That would let Renee know what she thinks in a nice way, be polite to Renee's grandma—and maybe make Renee think twice the next time she acts rude. ❏

ADVICE FROM KIDS

○ "When someone burps in class and tries to get me to laugh, I look the other way. Otherwise I might get blamed," says Andrew, 6.

○ "My friend Matt is so mean to his babysitter that I felt sorry for her. I told him he should be nicer to her and then she'll be nicer to him back. It worked!" offers Skip, 8.

○ "Don't let one friend say something bad about another friend. Instead, say, 'She's my friend just like you are, and I wouldn't let anyone talk that way about you,'" says Alice, 11.

Teach Your Child How To Make Others Comfortable

Thirteen-year-old Marcy is fairly outgoing, but she was still nervous about giving her first boy-girl party. "Think about the kids you invited," her dad suggested. "Who will feel shy? Who will stand around watching, feeling ignored? Concentrate on how you can help them join in!" It's good advice. When kids try to make another person feel more comfortable, a wonderful thing happens: they end up feeling more at ease and happier about themselves!

Be interested in others

An easy way for a child to make another child—or even an adult—feel good is to start a conversation with him or her. It doesn't matter if the other person is older or younger, boy or girl. The procedure is the same: start with a question.

According to Ann Marie Sabath, founder of AT EASE, INC., an etiquette school in Cincinnati, Ohio, when a child asks questions about the other person, he or she accomplishes two things. "First," Sabath explains, "the child learns something about the other person. And second, asking children—or adults—about themselves is one of the best ways to show we're interested in them."

Questions that require more than a one-word response, she says, keep a conversation going longer. For example, asking, "How was your trip to Florida?" "How did play rehearsal go?" or "How do you take care of your horse?" are better than "What's your favorite band?"

We can help kids develop conversation skills at home. Marcy's mom and dad, for example, play a conversation game at dinner once a week. Each of their kids has to come up with a question for each person at the table. At first, naturally, Marcy's dad had to remind them all to listen to the answers, but now, he says, "They hear their siblings out and don't interrupt." Other parents make suggestions before company comes, such as "Uncle Harry just bought a new car. Why don't you ask him about it?"

Questions not to ask

We all wince when our curious, forthright children ask visitors questions like "How much money do you make?" But if you tell kids which kinds of questions make people feel embarrassed and uncomfortable, most catch on fairly quickly. The topics to avoid include questions about money ("How much did this present cost?"), weight or personal appearance ("How much weight did you lose?" or "Do you dye your hair?"), sex ("Did you sleep together before you were married?"), and religion ("Do you think you're really drinking the blood of Christ every Sunday?").

Foster kindness

In order to be able to make people feel comfortable, kids need to be sensitive to others' feelings, be kind, and extend themselves for others. We often forget that they don't always know how to do these things. When two new girls joined Dania's fourth grade, Dania complained that they didn't even talk to anybody. "How do you think *you* would feel in a new school?" her mom countered. "Making them feel more welcome would be a kind thing for you to do." Her mom suggested these ideas:

- Use social cues: smile, wave, look them in the eye, and introduce yourself, and then introduce them to your friends.
- Invite them to sit with you on the bus or in the cafeteria.
- Offer to share something—a bag of potato chips, a book, a new game.
- Give a compliment—"I like your shirt."

- Ask about them, such as "Where are you from? Who have you met so far?"
- Invite them to your house after school.

Reaching out with kindness to others is always good manners, whether our kids defend a person being teased by others or call a sick friend who feels isolated from everything that's happening at school.

Awkward situations

We've all been in the awful situation of not knowing what to say to someone. When bad things happen, kids feel the same way. What do you say if your dad dies or your parents get divorced? In such situations a parent can help a child plan something simple to say to classmates, such as "My dad died and I'm feeling sad right now." If something bad happens to your child's friend—his parents divorce or he is in the hospital—you can suggest ways your child can comfort him by visiting or saying something sympathetic. Remember, even the smallest gesture will be appreciated. ❑

Teach Your Child Respect & Tolerance

An important part of teaching good manners is teaching our children to respect and be tolerant of people who are different from them—whether they are a different race, nationality, or religion; are special in terms of an emotional, mental, or physical impairment; are different in sexual orientation or economic background; or just wear different clothes, hairstyles, and like different kinds of music.

There are many reasons for teaching these kindnesses. For one, it encourages children to put themselves in another person's shoes and recognize that all human beings have value—which is at the heart of good manners. A child who knows the right fork to use but makes racial slurs has missed the whole point. This is an essential lesson for our kids to learn because the world they live in is becoming more and more diverse. By the time they are adults they will be working with and living among a much greater mix of races, nationalities, and alternative lifestyles than we do.

Tolerance at school

One place our kids are being challenged to practice tolerance is at school, as the policy of inclusion is established at more and more public schools throughout the country. The policy directs

schools to include *all* kids in regular elementary- and middle-school classrooms, even those severely mentally and/or physically disabled children who previously attended special education classes.

What inclusion means for kids is exposure to more differences in the classroom. In Judy's third grade is a boy who can't hear, so her class learned the sign language alphabet and some phrases to make him feel welcome. A girl in a wheelchair joined Andy's fifth grade, and students in that class take turns pushing her to special classes like music and art. In one second grade the students learned not to laugh at a boy with attention deficit disorder.

Some kids find learning to be tolerant of these children harder than others. But we can help by actively supporting the school's efforts and encouraging empathy in kids by asking them, as Andy's dad did, "How would you want to be treated by other children if you were in a wheelchair?"

Meeting "special" kids in the world

The more kids meet and get to know special kids, the more comfortable they feel around them. That happened to my daughter the year we attended the Special Olympics. The first time she saw a girl her own age in a wheelchair, she didn't want to look at her. "I feel so bad for her, Mom," she said. "I don't know what to say or do." Most kids feel the same way my daughter

did when confronted with children who are disabled.

The Special Olympics head volunteer explained that the best thing Annie could do was smile, look the girl in the eye, and say hello to her—then ask if she could take her to some of the events. Annie brightened. "Oh, I could do that," she said, and soon the two girls were applying face paint to each other's faces at one of the booths.

Once children are exposed to a special child they rapidly realize that kids are just kids after all, and they come to respect abilities and character traits just as they do with a regular child. As my daughter told me at the end of the day, "Boy, does Karen ever have strong arms! She could even pop a wheelie!"

Don't tease or make fun

Differences of any kind make many kids in elementary and middle school uncomfortable. One reason they make fun of or tease those who are different, like Luke, who's overweight, or Katrin, who has dyslexia and struggles with reading, is to make clear that they're not like them. Many of us have probably heard our own kids describe a classmate by saying, "He's a retard!" or "What a fatso!" or "She's a total klutz!"

Instead of just letting these comments go by, we can call kids on them as Wendy did when she overheard her son rudely mimic the accent of the checkout clerk at

ADVICE FROM KIDS

Kids with disabilities offer tips on how to treat them:

○ "Just 'cause I'm in a wheelchair, don't ignore me. Everyone tries not to stare, so in the halls no one looks me in the eye to say hello," complains Tom, 11.

○ "I get tired of looking up at everyone all day. Scrunch down so we're on the same level," says Lisa, 12.

○ "Talk about the same stuff you do with your other friends: TV shows or last night's homework," suggests Al, 13.

○ "Include me in some recess stuff. I may not be able to walk, but I can throw a ball," says Marla, 11.

the supermarket. "Sam," she said, "I heard that. What you just did was cruel and unkind and hurt that woman's feelings. I expect you to apologize."

Tolerance is also being kind

Tolerance also means actively showing kindness and sympathy for those who have difficult burdens to carry—a disability, unsightly birthmarks, a chronic illness—as well as for younger siblings who yearn to be included. Twelve-year-old Mary, for example, with a fair amount of parental prompting, now tolerates her younger sister's presence occasionally when her friends are over—they include her in their makeup and fingernail-painting sessions. Fortunately, she's thrilled to be the model.

How to treat older people

Like many parents, Mark, the father of two, believes that empathy, tolerance, and respect for others start with learning how to treat elderly relatives. "I expect my kids to defer to their grandparents," he says. "Running upstairs to get a pair of glasses, holding the door, and giving up the more comfortable chair in the living room are ways to show that respect."

It's not surprising that Mark's kids are also quick to open a door or give up a seat on the bus to an elderly person. "After all," they say, "I'd want someone to do that for my grandpa!"

Be an example

The song from the musical *South Pacific*, "You Have to Be Carefully Taught," which addresses racism and bigotry in children, explores the notion that you have to be "carefully taught" to hate a particular race, religion, or nationality—and that teaching generally comes from home. It's easy to forget that we teach children about tolerance every day through our own example. If we show our kids we respect others no matter what their race or religion, they probably will, too. And if we don't, we can be sure they will repeat our prejudices.

"The best way—and really the only way—to teach tolerance is to live it," explains Millie Willen, a clinical social worker on Long Island. Most important, she says, is making sure your kids see *you* behave with tolerance. To Barbara, mother of two, that means welcoming a new family to the neighborhood by inviting them to dinner regardless of their race, volunteering at a local nursing home, and holding doors for people who need it such as those in wheelchairs or with crutches. When she and her children watch TV together, she tries to point out and discuss racist, sexist, or ageist references that sometimes appear.

Another way we "live tolerance" is by not ignoring intolerance. If we laugh weakly when someone tells a racist or sexist joke, for example, it sends a message to our kids that such jokes are okay. ❑

YEAR BY YEAR
What To Expect At Different Ages

What To Expect At Different Ages— Manners & Social Skills

Between the ages of five and thirteen, children develop the good manners and social skills they will need and use for the rest of their lives. But learning manners is a gradual process, and parents find it easier to teach their kids if they match expectations with the appropriate age.

● *What all ages have in common.* All children, no matter what their age, can learn to show kindness and respect to others in some way. Knowing and using please, thank you, excuse me, hello, and good-bye are basics for every age group, as are good grooming and wearing appropriate clothes for special occasions. Children can master aspects of table manners, thank-you notes, sportsmanship, and other social skills, at each age. All kids are rude from time to time, both unintentionally *and* deliberately, and parents have to prompt and remind. Kids who don't know how to behave according to the standards for their age will have trouble when it comes to friendships and success in school.

● *What changes with age.* Parents—and the world at large—expect more from children in terms of manners and social skills as they grow older. One reason is that with each year children develop more self-control and empathy. At the same time, their social world widens, and more complex manners are required in situations, such as meeting others with different cultural backgrounds or attending boy-girl parties. What's considered rude behavior in a ten-year-old may be excused in a five-year-old. However, learning and using manners and social skills is not a smooth upward progression with clear age markers. Feeling at ease socially also partly depends on temperament, so an outgoing seven-year-old may act more polite with an adult than a shy ten-year-old does.

Ages 5 to 7

● *At home.* Many parents introduce manners basics when children are as young as two or three years old and continue to do so when they are in the early elementary-school grades. At these ages most kids are still very eager to please parents, but prompting and praise are necessary to reinforce the habits of saying please, thank you, and excuse me. By the end of first grade, children should be able to say hi or hello, look people in the eye, and shake hands or at least have a brief conversation when they meet adults.

As far as table manners go, this age group should be able to sit still for a dinner of at least twenty minutes. Most first graders can use a fork fairly easily, put their napkin on their lap, chew with their mouth closed, pass the bread basket, wait to start until they see the hostess pick up her fork, ask to be excused, and clear their plates. Interrupting others who are talking is common because kids so often get excited and forget. Calm reminders keep this from becoming a habit.

You can expect kids to learn how to answer the telephone by saying hello and following a script, as in "May I ask who's calling, please?" and "Just a minute, I'll get my mom." They can also understand why it's important not to interrupt and why listening on the extension is not okay.

● *Out in the world.* Going to school or preschool is when kids first move toward being part of society at large. Knowing some fundamental social skills helps them make that adjustment and get along with others. For example, saying hello can start friendships and saying please and thank you can win praise from teachers—as does adhering to the rules that are a big part of school. Being a good sport means not pouting or making excuses. By the age of seven, kids should be practicing some host and guest skills—greeting a playdate at the door, offering a snack, and giving him the first choice of what to do.

Most kids still dictate thank-you notes to a parent but should sign their names.

Ages 7 to 10

● *At home.* Children are more independent and social and have more empathy. At home as well as in school, they are eager to take on responsibility, act grown-up, and do the right thing. So they're ready to learn to make simple introductions, to speak when they're spoken to, to say, "You're welcome," to reply, "I'm fine, thanks," and to realize that making a friend feel comfortable in your own house takes thought and preparation. But this is also a big age for talking back, contradicting, and name-calling, which parents need to nip in the bud.

At the dinner table, younger kids can sit for thirty minutes, but fifth graders can make it through forty-five with relative ease. They can remember to come to the table with clean hands and face, cut their own meat neatly, pour juice for everyone, learn not to criticize the food, and place utensils properly when they're finished.

Most kids can use phone etiquette when calling friends.

● *Out in the world.* Kids this age spend more time away from their parents' supervision and are faced with many new social challenges. Sleepovers mean having to maneuver through different family rules and sometimes different cultural attitudes. Being a good host and a good guest become part of a more complex social system— kids are expected to make polite excuses, thank a friend's parent for having them over, play along and not complain at a party, and greet the driver of the car pool. They're ready to write their own thank-you notes, although they may make mistakes, and to show tact when they receive a present they don't like.

Audience manners become important because kids frequently attend assemblies, school plays, and go to movies. And as they become involved in competitive sports, they need to know the elements of good sportsmanship—friends will be quick to remind them even if you don't. Now is also the time to introduce the idea of holding doors for grown-ups and offering a seat to an older person who needs it.

Ages 10 to 13

● *At home.* These are the "polishing up" years for manners, when children consolidate what they've learned so far and extend the ways they show kindness and respect to others—calling a sick grandparent or being willing to entertain a visiting younger child. Parents usually see a split in how kids behave—one way with parents and other adults, another with peers. Insisting on good manners at home is still important, even though some kids resist mightily. Often they'll seek manners advice for special occasions, such as boy-girl parties, where they want to appear cool.

Personal appearance is critical to preteens, so parents find that grooming reminders aren't always necessary—in fact, it's hard to get some (but not all) adolescents *out* of the bathroom. However, expect fights over what constitutes appropriate attire. Some preteens think swearing is sophisticated, and need to be reminded not to criticize adults or tease classmates who are different. Telephone manners revolve around respecting time limits and remembering to take down accurate messages and relay them to others. Expect kids to be able to write longer thank-you notes.

● *Out in the world.* Preteens are judged more critically by adults in terms of manners and appearance and are expected to use such basics as please, thank you, and excuse me consistently. Some kids become shy, but they can learn to introduce themselves, make friends feel comfortable, and chat with adults. Their world now includes more activities, competitive sports, and the opposite sex. Peers are extremely important—and bad-mouthing and being a poor sport can cost kids friendships. As they start attending their own social functions, such as confirmation dinners, bar mitzvahs, and perhaps boy-girl events, they need to know formal table manners—this gives them confidence when they feel on display. They should also be able to ask for information or order food in a restaurant with poise.

Being out in the world for seventh and eighth graders also means doing such jobs as babysitting and yardwork, where using good manners is essential. ❏

WE RECOMMEND
Books, Games, Videos, & Manners Programs

BOOKS

For Kids in Elementary School

THE BERENSTAIN BEARS FORGET THEIR MANNERS
by Stan & Jan Berenstain (Random House, 1985)

In this humorous story, one of the best in the series, all the bears need to be more polite, even Papa Bear. Mama Bear comes up with a "Politeness Plan" chart. For kids four to eight years of age.

SOUP SHOULD BE SEEN, NOT HEARD: THE KIDS' ETIQUETTE BOOK
by Beth Brainard and Shelila Behr (Dell, 1990)

Besides basic etiquette for kids, this spiral-bound book with cartoon drawings also covers fish courses, crumbling crackers in soup, and proper dressy clothes. Despite the simple text, the book is appropriate for third through fifth graders.

PERFECT PIGS: AN INTRODUCTION TO MANNERS
by Marc T. Brown and Stephen Krensky (Little, Brown, 1983)

A picture book for kids up to second grade, this introduces very basic manners with colorful illustrations of pigs saying thank you and please.

IT'S A SPOON, NOT A SHOVEL
by Carolyn Buehner, Illustrations by Mark Buehner (Dial Books, 1995)

Beautiful full-page illustrations of animals with funny names, such as Arvin Anteater and Melissa Mandrel, demonstrating table manners make this a perfect manners lesson for kids in kindergarten through second grade.

CHARLIE AND THE CHOCOLATE FACTORY
by Roald Dahl (Knopf, 1964)

This magical story of a group of kids who tour a chocolate factory contrasts several nasty, repulsive children with polite and loyal Charlie. This is Dahl at his best. It was also made into a wonderful movie. Many fifth and sixth graders like it, too.

KIDSTORIES: BIOGRAPHIES OF 20 YOUNG PEOPLE YOU'D LIKE TO KNOW
by Jim Delisle (Free Spirit Publishing, 1991)

Aimed at third and fourth graders, this collection of true stories profiles kids who show more than good manners by doing something special to improve themselves, their schools, communities, or the world.

THE WIND IN THE WILLOWS
by Kenneth Grahame (St. Martin's Press, 1995)

In the beloved classic, Toad is a great example of a cad with no sense of propriety and Mr. Badger is the consummate mannerly English gentleman. This edition has new and wonderful illustrations.

CHILDREN JUST LIKE ME
by Barnabas and Anabel Kindersley (Dorling Kindersley, 1995)

The beautiful photographs of children from all over the world and fascinating information on their customs and lives make this a perfect book for discussing tolerance. For kids five through twelve.

WHAT DO YOU SAY, DEAR?/WHAT DO YOU DO, DEAR?
by Sesyle Joslin and Maurice Sendak (HarperTrophy, 1986)

In these two delightful books, the responses to what to say and do are set in hilarious situations, such as "What do you say when you bump into a crocodile on a busy street?" Both books are wonderfully instructive for the four-to-eight age group.

RICHARD SCARRY'S PLEASE & THANK YOU BOOK
by Richard Scarry (Random House, 1973)

An extensive range of manners—from table manners to visiting manners to recess and safety manners—are all shown in charming illustrations. Stories about the two pigs—Pig Will and Pig Won't—under-score the importance of cooperation. Just terrific! For preschool through grade two.

For Kids in Middle School

THE MOVES MAKE THE MAN
By Bruce Brooks (Harper/Trophy, 1984)

Two thirteen-year-olds—a black basketball player and an emotionally troubled white shortstop—form a precarious friendship in North Carolina. This Newbery Honor winner examines sportsmanship and tolerance in adolescent boys.

CHILDREN OF THE RIVER
By Linda Crew (Dell, 1989)

A thirteen-year-old flees her native Cambodia and, four years later, struggles to fit in at her Oregon high school. The novel, which won the Children's Book Award in 1989, compares and contrasts the diverse manners, traditions, and social customs of the two very different countries. For kids in grades seven and eight.

A POCKET BOOK OF MANNERS FOR YOUNG PEOPLE
by Elizabeth Hammond (Trotwood Press, 1990)

Though intended for kids in fourth through eighth grades, this short paperback can also be used by early readers as a reference book. It illustrates one rule of manners per page.

OOPS! THE MANNERS GUIDE FOR GIRLS
by Nancy Holyoke (American Girl Library, Pleasant Company, 1997)

A comprehensive manners guide for girls ages eight to twelve, this book covers much more than such basic topics as table manners. One chapter, "Yikes: Embarrassing Moments," discusses what's "gross" and another, "Big Days," tells what to do at weddings, family parties, and sleepovers.

SOCIAL SMARTS: MANNERS FOR TODAY'S KIDS
by Elizabeth James and Carol Barkin (Clarion Books, 1996)

Rather than basic etiquette, this book focuses mainly on social skills for specific life situations such as parties, school, sleepovers, and hospital visits. A chapter on "Difficult Times" addresses the tough subjects of dealing with death and serious illness with sensitivity and grace.

EMILY POST'S TEEN ETIQUETTE
*by Elizabeth Post and Joan M. Coles
(HarperCollins, 1995)*

An up-to-date Emily Post book directed at young teens, this guide includes how to handle call-waiting, beepers, and e-mail as well as more traditional rules of etiquette.

SOCIAL SAVVY: A TEENAGER'S GUIDE TO FEELING CONFIDENT IN ALL SITUATIONS
*by Judith Ré with Meg F. Schneider
(Simon & Schuster, 1991)*

Aimed at early adolescents as well as teens, this book gives practical step-by-step answers to sticky situations, like what to do when your meatball torpedoes off the plate or you can't remember someone's name, what to do when you walk into a party and don't know anyone, and how to say no politely but firmly.

For Parents

LETITIA BALDRIGE'S MORE THAN MANNERS!
by Letitia Baldrige (Rawson Associates, 1997)

The author concentrates on teaching children kindness, harmony, teamwork, selflessness, and compassion as social skills and incorporates them into the more traditional rules of children's etiquette.

TEACHING YOUR CHILD THE LANGUAGE OF SOCIAL SUCCESS
by Marshall P. Duke, Stephen Nowicki, Jr., and Elisabeth A. Martin (Peachtree, 1996)

Although not officially a manners guide, this book looks at how your child's social success is linked to his ability to read and use nonverbal language. The writers assess social skills by examining body language, posture, facial expressions, and tone of voice.

RAISING A RESPONSIBLE CHILD
*By Elizabeth M. Ellis, Ph.D.
(Birch Lane Press, 1995)*

A clinical psychologist explains how to teach kids to become independent and self-sufficient. In easy-to-understand language, Ellis gives tips on many manners issues—handling an adolescent's telephone privileges, young children's eating habits, and much more.

THE WONDER OF BOYS
by Michael Gurian (Tarcher/Putman, 1997)

This book describes what boys need to become responsible, sensitive, courteous men without compromising their natural propensity for competition and aggression. The section on teaching boys values and social codes also addresses morality, discipline, and behavior for specific situations.

DEAR MS. DEMEANOR
by Mary Mitchell (Contemporary Books, 1995)

Nationally syndicated advice columnist Mitchell uses letters she has received from teens to address social skills at home and in public. Through the question-and-answer style she offers common-sense advice for difficult situations. Each section of letters on a topic is preceded by advice for parents. It's a sensible guide for families and mature seventh and eighth graders.

The Family That Works Together
by Lynn Lott (Prima Publishing, 1995)

This practical guide teaches families how to work together courteously and cheerfully to accomplish family chores.

Positive Discipline for Single Parents:
A Practical Guide to Raising Children Who Are Responsible, Respectful, and Resourceful
by Jane Nelson, Cheryl Erwin, and Carol Delzer (Prima Publishing, 1994)

Single parents will appreciate the ideas on raising polite kids despite the difficulties of being the only one in charge. There are good chapters on stepfamily social skills and divorced family gatherings.

GAMES

Mind Your Manners
(board game)

Two to six players answer questions from one of fifty-two categories, such as "which fork to use" and "how to make proper introductions." This is an informative and entertaining way for kids to learn greetings, telephone manners, guest manners, and more. (For ages seven and up. To order, call 800/873-9909; $28.00 + shipping.)

Manners-In-A-Flash

Twelve different sets of twenty flash cards each quiz kids on a variety of etiquette topics—restaurant manners, travel manners, school manners, etc. (To order, call 800/ 873-9909; $18.75 per title + shipping.)

VIDEOS

A Kid's Guide to Manners

The importance of being polite and why parents and teachers are so concerned about manners are the subjects of this award-winning, animated etiquette guide for elementary-school kids. (To order, call 800/873-9909; $85.00 + shipping.)

Babe *(1995)*

An amazing live-action barnyard fable about social tolerance. Characters include a collie family, a nervous duck, and piglet Babe, who, by learning compassion and social skills, wins a sheepdog contest. Great for the whole family.

My Fair Lady *(1964)*

In this classic family musical, Eliza Doolittle, an ill-mannered flower girl, becomes a "lady" after elocution and etiquette training by Professor Henry Higgins. In the end, it is Eliza who reminds upper-class Higgins to practice basic human kindness toward all classes of people.

The Karate Kid *(1984)*

A young teenager learns to cope with bullies by learning from an unlikely mentor, a middle-aged Japanese handyman, who teaches him respect and courage. Kids learn a bit about formal Japanese etiquette including the traditional tea ceremony. Rated R for language, but still appropriate for kids in junior high.

MARY POPPINS *(1964)*

A practically perfect nanny brings about profound change in the Banks family. Her charges learn courtesy and respect towards others. Wonderful music, too.

CROSSED SWORDS *(1978)*

There are several versions of this Mark Twain classic tale of two boys—one a young prince and the other a street urchin—who look so much alike that they trade places for a while. Each learns the manners, culture, and customs of his new "class." Basic human courtesy is exalted. *Crossed Swords* is for kids ten and up.

WILLY WONKA AND THE CHOCOLATE FACTORY *(1971)*

A terrific look at the power and effects of showing good manners and what happens when you don't, this adaptation of the Ronald Dahl book, *Charlie and the Chocolate Factory,* tells the story of five kids who tour a chocolate factory.

LITTLE PRINCESS *(1995)*

Remake of the Shirley Temple classic in which an indulged girl, having lived in India with her free-spending father, is uprooted to a grim New York City boarding school. There are bits on table manners and proper Victorian behavior. Even eight-year-olds like this film, girls especially.

MASK *(1985)*

The ultimate film about acceptance, this story about a sixteen-year-old boy with a disfiguring bone disease really shows kids what it's like to be different. Good scenes depict right and wrong behavior by classmates and teachers. For kids ten and up.

MANNERS PROGRAMS

AT EASE, INC.

Ann Marie Sabath heads this etiquette program for adults and children. She also offers a program that fullfills the Girl Scout etiquette badge requirements. (Call 800/873-9909 or write to 119 East Court Street, Cincinnati, OH 45202.)

THE CHILDREN'S SPOON™

Paula Person founded her educational program to revitalize social manners for all children and to build kids' self-confidence. She teaches groups of children around the country. (Call 847/251-3382 or write to P.O. Box 148, Winnetka, IL 60093.)

JUDITH RÉ ACADEMIE

Judith Ré has been teaching seminars on etiquette in schools and corporations since 1986. (Call 203/330-9199 or write to 147 Algonquin Rd., Fairfield, CT 06432.)

RITZ KIDS

Basic etiquette for children ages eight to fourteen is offered by most Ritz-Carlton Resorts in the U.S. and two in the Caribbean as part of the children's program during school holidays and in summer. (Check on specific hotels by calling 800/241-3333.) ❏